Art Buchwald

HAVE I EVER LIED TO YOU?

A FAWCETT CREST BOOK
Fawcett Publications, Inc., Greenwich, Conn.
Member of American Book Publishers Council, Inc.

INTRODUCTION

Art Buchwald works in a small airless room on the top of the Washington Monument. Subsisting on nothing but orange juice and black coffee, Mr. Buchwald writes his column in longhand on the backs of old White House press releases. They are then attached to the legs of speedy pigeons and delivered to the 421 newspapers that carry his column to every part of the civilized and uncivilized world.

From his view on the top of the monument, Buchwald is able to see everything that is going on in the nation's capital. His sharp eyes pierce the curtains of the Executive Mansion, the Pentagon, the FBI, and, of course, the CIA. Shy, introspective and terribly aloof, Mr. Buchwald rarely leaves his room except to buy *Time* Magazine to see if they've put him on the cover.

Despite his long years in Washington, Mr. Buchwald is still a mystery to fellow newspapermen. Some say that Art Buchwald is a pseudonym and the column is written by the Joint Chiefs of Staff—each service taking the duty for one month. Another theory is that Art Buchwald is really Howard Hughes, which, if true, would make him the richest columnist in the country today. A third theory is that Art Buchwald is really Dlawhcub Tra spelled backward.

THE PUBLISHERS

※ ※ ※ ※ ※

A Fawcett Crest Book reprinted by arrangement with G. P. Putnam's Sons.

Library of Congress Catalog Card Number: 68–15500

Printing History
G. P. Putnam's Sons edition published April 1968
First printing, January 1968
Second printing, March 1968
Third printing, April 1968

First Fawcett Crest printing, April 1969

Published by Fawcett World Library
67 West 44th Street, New York, New York 10036
Printed in the United States of America

CONTENTS

4   Live and In Color

5   One-Eyed Moshe

6   I Want a Paper Doll

7   E-E-E-E-Konomics

8   No Dropout, He—

9   Hey, There!

10   Keep the Faith, Baby

11   Will the Real Mao Please Stand Up?

1

�an ✱ ✱ ✱ ✱ ✱ ✱ ✱ ✱ ✱ ✱ ✱ ✱ ✱

WHO'S WORRIED?

DID HERSHEY DO RIGHT?

General Louis B. Hershey has decided to draft all students who are against the draft. While this is a noble idea, I think he's asking for more trouble than it's worth.

We take you to Camp Loakum, the basic training camp nearest to Berkeley, where a drill sergeant has been called in by his colonel to explain why his platoon doesn't seem to be showing too much military acumen.

"Sergeant, your platoon has the worst record of any platoon on this base. How do you explain it?"

"It's not my fault, sir. It's General Hershey's. He drafted all these antidraft draftees, and they're driving me up the wall."

"How?"

"Well, to give you an example, the other morning I came in the barracks and announced we were going on a twenty-mile hike. They all started chanting, 'Hell, no! We won't go! Hell, no! We won't go!' I got mad and started to kick their butts in, so they all stretched out on the floor and announced they were holding a lie-in. Every time I called attention, they went limp. I tell you, sir, it's driving me out of my mind."

"Haven't you threatened them with punishment?"

"It doesn't do any good. When I threaten them, they accuse me of having a sadistic military mind, but they insist they love me."

"What?" the colonel splutters.

"Yes, sir. They say they love me, and whenever I kick their butts in, they give me a daffodil."

"Where the hell do they get daffodils?" the colonel shouts.

"Their friends send them to them. The other day we were out on the bayonet course and they started handing out daffodils to another platoon. I've been the laughingstock of the base ever since."

The colonel says, "I'll admit it sounds as if you've got problems."

"You don't know what problems are, sir. On the drill field when we're marching in cadence, instead of shouting, 'Left, right, left, right,' they yell, 'Make love, not war, make love,

10

not war.' It just doesn't sound right from a military point of view, does it, sir?"

"I shouldn't think it does."

"The other night I handed out PX cards, and you know what they did? They burned them. I've been buying soap for them out of my own money ever since."

"That's good thinking, Sergeant. What's that you're holding in your hand?"

"Those are petitions, sir. This one was drawn up by the Committee to Legalize VD, this one is the Ad Hoc Committee to Get Our Boys out of Camp Loakum, and this one I'd rather not say."

"What do you mean you'd rather not say? What is it?"

"Well, sir, this one is a petition to try you for war crimes."

"War crimes?"

"Yes, sir. They've called a mass meeting at three o'clock in front of camp headquarters, and they're going to burn you in effigy."

"I think I'd better call General Hershey and ask him to reconsider his last order," the colonel says.

"That's a good idea, sir. I'd better get back to the platoon. When I left them, they said they wouldn't make up their beds until General Westmoreland apologized to Senator Fulbright."

TOO OLD TO WORK

The trouble with the American Dream these days is that there has been such an emphasis on youth in our country that a man can be washed up at the age of forty and not even know it. I didn't realize how serious it was getting until I started trying to find some jobs for friends who were victims of the *World Journal Tribune* closing.

The first question people would ask me was, "How old is he?" If I said he was forty or older, I'd get a shrug and some comment like, "He's too old for us."

It seems to me that if the trend continues, the age gap is going to be one of the most serious problems this country faces. It's quite possible in another ten or fifteen years that the following scene might become very common.

PERSONNEL MANAGER: "I see your qualifications are in order except for one thing."

APPLICANT: "What's that?"

PERSONNEL MANAGER: "I'm afraid you're too old for the job."

APPLICANT: "What do you mean 'too old for the job'? I'm twenty-three."

PM: "Yes, I see that. We don't hire anyone over twenty-one years of age."

APPLICANT: "But I just got out of college. I've never had a job. How can I be too old?"

PM: "According to our pension planners, who have the final say on how old our employees should be, anybody above twenty-one years of age is over the hill."

APPLICANT: "How can I be over the hill if I've never been on?"

PM: "There's no reason to get testy about this. We have nothing personal against you. It's just that we have found through experience that men of your age really don't do their best work when they reach twenty-three or twenty-four years of age. Oh, there have been exceptions, but on the whole, we'd rather take our chances with the younger man who can stand up under the physical and mental pressures of the job."

APPLICANT: "I appreciate your thinking, but I can assure you I can do anything a twenty-one-year-old can do. I'm still very strong. I play tennis twice a week. I'm in excellent health, and I was even captain of my football team last year."

PM: "Sir, I don't doubt everything you say, but we can't judge you as an individual. Statistics show your age group is prone to colds, backaches, and bursitis. Even if we wanted to hire you, our group health insurance advisers wouldn't let us. They can't afford to take the risk with a twenty-three-year-old man, no matter how healthy he may look."

APPLICANT: "But if I can't get a job now that I've finished college, what am I going to do the rest of my life?"

PM: "Why don't you retire and move to Florida?"

APPLICANT: "What the hell am I going to retire on if I never worked?"

PM: "That's not our fault, is it? Don't forget, this company is in a fiercely competitive market, and if we hire older people like yourself, we'll have to explain it to our stockholders. Besides, it looks bad when a customer comes in and sees a twenty-three-year-old man hunched over his desk."

APPLICANT: "I hate to beg, but I really need this job. This

is the fourth company I've been to which says I'm too old. Please, mister, give me a chance. I still have ten good years in me."

PM: "I'm sorry, sir. I don't wish to be cold-hearted about this, but I think you should face reality. You're washed up. You should have planned for your old age years ago."

APPLICANT: "Let me ask one more question and then I'll go. How old are you?"

PERSONNEL MANAGER: "Thirteen."

WHY PARENTS ARE AFRAID

Many colleges these days demand that any student seeking admittance submit to a personal interview, as well as take the entrance examinations. While most teen-agers can absorb such interviews in stride, their parents turn into Jello at the thought of taking them around to various campuses.

I didn't realize the psychological scars such interviews leave on fathers until I accompanied my friend Luckhauser and his lovely daughter, Linda, to a fancy school in Pennsylvania.

On the drive up, Luckhauser was trying to put his daughter at ease. "Look, honey, I want to prepare you for the worst. It may not be your fault if they say no, and I want you to know I won't think any less of you if you don't get in."

"Okay, Pops," Linda said as she looked up from her crossword puzzle.

"In life we must be ready for rejection," Luckhauser continued. "Many times the people who reject us do it because they have been rejected themselves."

"Okay, Pops," Linda said. "What's a three-letter word for crazy?"

"I hoped you'd pay more attention to me," Luckhauser said angrily.. "This interview could change your whole life. I wish there was a store where you could buy the questions they ask you."

"Luckhauser," I said, "you're more nervous than Linda. Why don't you just cool it, or you'll get her as upset as you are?"

"You can say that," Luckhauser replied, as he almost hit a

truck, "but you're not her father. It isn't easy for a parent to see his child being judged by a complete stranger."

We finally arrived at the administration building. Luckhauser was shaking with fear as I led him up the steps to the director of admissions' office. Linda was holding his other arm.

The secretary had us sit on a long wooden bench, and in fifteen minutes she said, "Miss Luckhauser, you can go in now."

Luckhauser got up to go in with his daughter, and the secretary said, "I'm sorry, Mr. Luckhauser, the interview is a private one just with your daughter."

"There's probably a lot of things I know about Linda that she doesn't even know," Luckhauser said, edging toward the door.

The secretary was stern. "Just Linda, please."

I pulled Luckhauser down on the bench.

"See you later, Pops," Linda said as she went in the door.

Ten minutes later Luckhauser was pacing up and down. "What's taking them so long? If they don't want her, why don't they just tell her and let us get out of here?"

"Luckhauser," I said, "it's only been ten minutes. These interviews last at least forty minutes."

"She's weak in math. I think she should tell them that. We never said she was good in math."

"They probably know that," I said.

"But she was on the school newspaper. Worked her heart out. I hope she remembers to tell them that. Maybe I could send in a note to remind her to tell them."

"Leave well enough alone, Luckhauser. Linda can handle herself."

"She's too modest. She never talks about herself," he said. "I should have briefed her before she went in."

"Here," I said. "Read a magazine and relax."

"You know," he said in a loud voice so that the secretary could hear, "there are a lot of schools that are after Linda. I would hate to have to make her decision where she really wants to go."

A half hour later Luckhauser was tearing the felt out of his hat. "Why doesn't she come out? What are they doing to her?"

Linda and the director of admissions finally came out. Luckhauser jumped up. "Well?"

"We'll let you know in April," the director said.

"April?" Luckhauser cried. "I'll never be able to wait that long."

DOWN WITH MOTHER'S DAY

As soon as President Johnson announced that May 8 would be Mother's Day, the Coordinating Committee of the Nonviolent Students Against Mothers opened up headquarters in Washington.

The chairman of the committee, Charley La Barbe, held a press conference and protest meeting, to which I was invited.

The headquarters was filled with people making signs and banners—"Get Out of Mother's Day," "Take Mothers to the UN," "Why Be a Mother When You Can Take a Pill?"

La Barbe said that his committee had caught on like wildfire, particularly among students who hated their mothers.

I saw a large crowd on the steps, and I asked La Barbe what one of the students was doing.

"He's burning his birth certificate."

"That takes a lot of guts," I said.

"We're going to have the biggest demonstration this country has ever seen," he said. "Do you know what we're doing Sunday?"

"I'd hate to guess."

"We're hanging Whistler's mother in effigy."

"Who are those women over there?"

"That's our Mother's Committee Against Mothers. They'll be protesting with their children on May 8."

"Your movement seems to be snowballing," I said.

"There are a lot of people in this country who are to be heard from," he said. "Everyone is afraid to speak out against motherhood because it's unpatriotic to demonstrate."

"This is a personal question, but why are you against your mother?"

"Because I was tricked. I served in World War II, and we were told that one of the things we were fighting for was Ma's apple pie. Well, I came home after the war and asked my mother to make me an apple pie. Do you know something? It wasn't worth fighting for."

"Was it the crust or the apples?" I asked him.

"Both. She finally went out and bought a frozen pie. Four years I fought, and all I got out of it was a frozen apple pie."

"So that's when you got your idea to abolish Mother's Day?"

"That isn't the only thing. She wouldn't let me watch television while I was going to college.

"But I'm not putting this on a personal level. Johnson isn't telling us the whole truth about Mother's Day. He expects us to go along with him on May 8, but he refuses to say how far he's going to get involved and how many mothers he's going to commit."

"Do you plan to hold a peaceful demonstration?"

"We do unless the cops give us trouble. The fuzz are all mother lovers, you know."

"What happens if you get arrested?"

"Our mothers have all promised to bail us out."

THE PROUD PARENTS

A lot of proud parents show up the month of June at university commencement exercises throughout the land. I was sitting next to a beaming couple, and during the ceremonies I struck up a conversation.

"You must be very happy today," I said to the father.

"Oh, I am. Martha and I have waited all our lives for this moment when Peter would graduate from college."

"Which one up there is Peter?"

"He's not there," the father replied. "He walked out when Secretary McNamara started to make the commencement speech."

"That's a shame," I said. "I guess you and your wife are pretty upset."

"Oh, no. He told us he originally planned to lie down across the podium, so we're very grateful he decided on a nonviolent protest."

"I'll bet you scrimped and saved to put Peter through college."

"Actually, the tuition wasn't too bad. We had set funds aside for that. But it was pretty hard to get up the bail money every time Peter got arrested. We managed though, except for the time he burned his draft card."

"He had to stay in jail for that one?"

"I'm afraid so. It wasn't just burning his draft card that got the administration angry—Peter accidentally burned down the gym with it."

"It must have played heck with the basketball schedule," I said.

"It did. But when Peter got out, he started a freedom committee to burn down gymnasiums, and about a fourth of the school signed up."

"What did Peter major in while he was in college?"

"He started out majoring in modern anarchy, but he found it was too restrictive, so he took a straight liberal arts course with a minor in Nietzsche. Martha wanted him to study law, but Peter said, 'There are no laws.' And that was the end of it."

"Peter sounds as if he's got a mind of his own."

"I think you could say that. He's the only one in his class who stopped two troop trains going in opposite directions at the same time on the Atchison, Topeka, and the Santa Fe."

"You have to have convictions to do that," I said.

"You also have to have long legs," the father said. "Peter then walked from Anchorage to Nome, Alaska, because he claimed the Alaskans wouldn't let the Eskimos vote. And he also sat in Governor Romney's office for two nights as a protest against capital punishment."

"But Michigan doesn't have capital punishment."

"That's what Governor Romney kept telling him."

"It must have been an interesting four years for you."

"I guess you could say that, particularly during school vacations when Peter found it hard to get LSD."

"Now that Peter's finished college, what does he plan to do?" I asked.

"He's applied for training jobs with IBM, Time-Life Inc., and the Ford Motor Company. He figures there's a much better future with a large corporation than trying to start out on your own."

THE STUDENT WHO CAME IN FROM THE COLD

It was bound to happen that the CIA would come to be blamed for everything. The other day a friend of mine received a very unfavorable report on his son's college grades. When the son came home for the weekend, his father decided to call him on it.

"This is the worst report I've ever seen," the father said.

"It's not my fault. I was ordered to get low grades so the other kids would trust me."

"Who ordered you?"

"I can't say, but if you knew, you'd be proud of me."

"Well, I'm not proud of you. It says here you've cut classes thirty-five times in the past three months, that you've been seen in bars every night, and that you were caught twice trying to get into the girls' dormitory."

"Somebody's got to do the dirty work if this country's going to remain strong. It's all right to say we've got to play by the rules, but the other side isn't playing by the rules."

"What other side?"

"Never mind what other side. It's kids like me that are saving people like you from slave labor camps."

"Don't give me that double talk," the father said angrily. "It says in the report that you cheated on three exams."

"To the school it's cheating; to me it's using every means to achieve my democratic goals. In a life-and-death struggle you can't play by the Marquess of Queensbury rules."

"All right, but what about these three drunk driving charges?"

"I was following another student's car, and he was drunk. Since I was weaving, too, the police thought I was drunk as well."

"Didn't they give you a sobriety test?"

"Yes, but I had taken several drinks just before I was caught so the other student wouldn't know I was following him. It will all come out in Allen Dulles' next book if you'll just be patient."

"I've heard some cock-and-bull stories in my time, but this

takes the cake. The dean of men said you were also involved in an off-campus LSD party which turned into an orgy."

"Well, you're not going to learn anything in the school library, at least not anything of importance. There were certain people who wanted me to go to that party. My attendance was approved by the highest echelons of our government. You don't think I'd go to an off-campus orgy on my own?"

"I don't know what to think anymore."

"The trouble is that the school reports only on my failures, but they're duty-bound not to say anything about my successes. If you ask me, they're making a tempest out of a teapot."

"I'd like to make a tempest out of your teapot," the father said. "The report winds up saying that it doubts, on the basis of your behavior, that it wants you to return to school."

"It's all a plot, Dad. Didn't you see *The Spy Who Came In from the Cold*? I'm supposed to be discredited by everybody so the other side will ask me to come over to their side. The school's kicking me out into the cold just like they did to Richard Burton in the movie."

"Do you mind telling me who the other side is?"

"They haven't told me yet. I suppose it's Harvard."

THERE IS NO BREAD

Sometime ago Stokely Carmichael told the students at Fisk University in Nashville to take over the school. There have been similar suggestions made by radical speakers on other campuses, and it's hard for an outsider to figure out what exactly the far-out students would do if they did take over the school. Perhaps it would go something like this.

"Hey, man, we are now in complete charge of Banana University. Since it was my idea, I'm the new chancellor."

"Crazy. I'm the president, Dirty Eddie is the new dean of men, Clara is the dean of women, and Papa Pete is dean of medicine."

"Hey, Chancellor, there's a bunch of kids outside who want to know when classes are going to begin."

"Tell them they can start anytime they want to."

"But there are no professors left. They all took off when you took over."

"Well, get some graduate students to teach them. They're on our side."

"The graduate students say they won't start teaching until they see some bread."

"We don't have any bread."

"I got it, Chancellor. Let's charge tuition and use that to pay the instructors."

"That's a good idea, Dirty Eddie. You announce it to the students. Tell 'em we need tuition to pay the teachers so classes can start again."

Dirty Eddie comes back in a few minutes. "The students wouldn't listen to me. They said we are part of the reactionary administration now, and they're going to hang us all in effigy. The student newspaper has come out with an extra attacking our high-handed attitude in dealing with their demands."

"What are their demands?"

"They don't know. They said if we were sensitive to their feelings, *we'd* know what they should demand."

"Clara, you go out and talk to them. Maybe you can find out what they want."

Clara returns. "They're holding a rally now to demand our resignations. They said there will never be peace on campus until they have a say in the running of the school."

"But we represent them."

"Not anymore, we don't. David and Bathsheba have started a new organization called Students Against the Student Administration. They said we have to negotiate with them, or they're going to boycott our antidraft rally tomorrow."

"Oh, they are, are they? Well, we'll see about that. Get me the campus chief of police . . . Chief, this is Chancellor, here. The students are holding an unauthorized rally on the promenade. I want your men to break it up and arrest the ringleaders. Yes, use police dogs and billy clubs if you have to, and call in the National Guard only if it's absolutely necessary."

"Chancellor, the students have just set fire to your motorcycle."

"That does it. I'm going to resign. If that's all they care about higher education, they don't deserve a decent administration."

"We'll all resign. Let David and Bathsheba have the headaches of running this place."

"You said it. I'd rather be back on LSD anyway."

"Wouldn't we all?"

FREE SPEECH FOR EVERYONE

The free speech movements on various campuses have become more militant in recent months, and I naturally was interested to know what they were up to. So I went over to the Sitdown Institute of Technology to confer with an organization called the Students for Utterly Free Speech and the Preservation of Democratic Institutions Through the Exchange of Ideas Movement.

The young man in charge of the organization was very happy to speak to me.

"Sir," I said, "what is the purpose of the Students for Utterly Free Speech?"

"Our main purpose is to keep speakers who come to college campuses from speaking."

"That's a very idealistic goal," I said. "How do you do this?"

"It's quite simple. When the speaker starts talking, we begin to heckle and shout at him so he can't be heard. The more he persists, the noisier we get, and pretty soon everyone is shouting, and if we're lucky, it turns into a brawl."

"This probably sounds like a stupid question, but if your organization is presumably for free speech, why don't you let the speaker say what he has on his mind?"

"But we're not for free speech for the *speaker!* We're for free speech for ourselves. We demand the right to interrupt anybody anytime he opens his mouth. This is still a democratic country, and we have a right to prevent anyone we want from speaking."

"But if you don't hear what the speaker has to say, how do you know you disagree with him?"

"We know we disagree with him before he comes. Anything he says might just confuse us. We're not fools, you know."

"I didn't say you were," I said. "But let's say, for argument's sake, that a speaker may have something new to add to the debate. Don't you think he should be able to put forth his position at the university?"

"None of the speakers has anything new to say. Besides, if we let one speaker put forth his arguments, then we'd have to let other speakers put forth their arguments, and pretty soon you'd have all sorts of ideas floating around, and it would hurt the free speech movement."

"How could it hurt the free speech movement?"

"Well, our members don't want to sit around listening to people making a lot of speeches all day. They like action. That's why they joined the free speech movement. We prefer to boo and shout a lot. It gets rid of our hostilities."

"I can see that. But on the other hand, look at it from the speaker's point of view. He's probably worked on his speech for several days, taken time off to come to the university. Shouldn't he be allowed to talk?"

"It's not our fault he went to all that trouble. If he were smart, he would have just written the opening lines of his speech, and we would have seen to it that no one knew that was all he had to say. We'll cooperate with a speaker if he cooperates with us."

"Is there any situation where you would allow a speaker to finish his speech?"

"We don't like to make exceptions, but I guess if he used four-letter words, we might let him finish. You see, our free speech movement believes we should be allowed to use four-letter words."

"How do four-letter words contribute to the cause of free speech?"

"It helps us understand the exchange of ideas."

WHY ARE WE THERE?

If a reporter can't cover the war in Vietnam, he can do the next best thing and cover the war on the campus of the University of California at Berkeley.

As my helicopter circled the scarred Zone D area, where a major battle had taken place between the bearded insurgent guerrilla forces of Mario Savio and the university special forces of Chancellor Roger Heyns, I knew I had two questions I wanted answered. One was, "Should the United States pull out of Berkeley?" and two was, "Should the Americans be there in the first place?"

Until you've been to Berkeley, it's hard to understand the enormous problems that we are confronted with out there. Although the administration still holds some of the major buildings; the sidewalks, the Union, and most of the steps are controlled by the students; and nonstudent infiltration is becoming so serious that some authorities are talking about planting mines in the parking lot adjacent to the school.

If you talk to the university people stationed in Sproul Hall, you get the impression that the administration is winning the war.

"It's true," a spokesman said, "that our pacification program is not working as well as we would hope it to, and many of the students and instructors in outlying colleges are afraid to go out at night. But we have more students in classes now than we did in 1964, and the insurgents know they can't drive us out."

But it is only when you go out into the field that you get a true picture of what is going on in Berkeley. I spoke to a grizzled veteran of the First Free Speech Movement Brigade, who was dug in behind a park bench on the outskirts of the campus.

He said, "You ask why are we fighting? We are fighting for freedom for students everywhere. We are fighting for our mothers and fathers and the girl next door so they can use four-letter words and smoke pot and take trips with LSD and have meaningful love experiences without fear and retribution. On these points there is no room for negotiation. The administration has to get out and leave the Cal students to run their own affairs."

"Does that mean the professors, too?"

"It means every foreign element. They have been bombing us with tests and strafing us with lectures and threatening us with expulsion. But for every atrocity they commit, we have burned down a draft card and will continue to do so until our cause is won."

He gave me a safe-conduct pass to visit the Third Psychedelic Division, who were holed up in an apartment right off the campus. The commander offered me a cube of sugar and apologized because he didn't have any tea to go with it.

"What do you miss most out here?" I asked him.

"The Los Angeles Dodgers, Debbie Reynolds, and Mom's

apple pie. But somebody's got to fight the fuzz, and I would rather it be me than my kid brother."

I toured the northern part of the campus where I found elements of the Sixty-fifth Sexual Freedom Battalion, sacked out next to their Hondas. A weary nineteen-year-old kid said, "There will never be peace at Berkeley until they permit our coeds to wear topless cheerleader uniforms at the football stadium."

I finally found an atheist in a foxhole—six to be exact. One of them said, "If there was a God, he'd be on our side."

As for whether the United States should be in Berkeley or not, I came away with the impression that it was a mistake for us to get involved there in the first place, but now that we're committed, we might as well stay, at least until midterm exams.

YES, WE HAVE BANANAS

It's very hard to be a parent of a teen-ager these days. You have to keep on your toes all the time. Just the other morning I walked into the kitchen and I caught my son taking a banana out of the fruit bowl.

"What are you doing with that banana?" I shouted.

"I'm going to cut it up and put it on my cereal," he replied.

"A likely story," I said. "You weren't going to smoke it, were you?"

"Smoke the cereal?"

"No, smoke the banana, smart aleck. I read all about you kids going around smoking bananas behind your parents' backs for kicks."

He became very interested. "How do you smoke a banana?" he wanted to know.

"You don't smoke the banana. You smoke the skin."

He looked at me in amazement. "What have you been smoking?"

"Now don't try to be smart with me," I said. "You know very well what I'm talking about. You take the skin and scrape it out, and then make a paste out of it, and then you bake it, and then you smoke it."

"What for?"

"So you'll have hallucinations, that's what for. First it was marijuana, then it was LSD, and now it's bananas. Don't you have any shame?"

"Look, all I want to do is have breakfast. I'll eat the fruit, and you can keep the skin if it bugs you that much."

"How do I know you didn't scrape off the skin before I came in?" I said.

"Search me," he yelled.

Just then my wife walked in to find out what the commotion was all about.

"I caught him eating a banana," I said.

"Well, what's wrong with that?" she demanded.

"Don't you read the newspapers? Kids all over the country are smoking bananas so they can take trips."

"Take trips where?"

"Wherever bananas will take them."

My wife looked scared. "Are you feeling all right?"

"Why does everyone think I'm crazy because I don't want my kids to smoke bananas?" I cried.

"Well, if you feel that strongly about it," she said, "I won't buy any bananas again."

"Sure, and then they'll sneak up to the fruit store and buy them behind our backs. At least this way we know they're getting good-quality bananas."

"Why don't we let him smoke a banana in front of us to get it out of his system?" my wife suggested.

"I don't want to smoke a banana," my son yelled. "In fact, I don't even want to eat my cornflakes."

"That's a good idea. We'll all smoke bananas together, and that way we'll know what the kids are experiencing. You're lucky you have modern parents."

I started scraping out the skins and making a paste. Then I baked it, and then I chopped it up and passed out three pipes.

The three of us sat around the floor of the living room and started to puff.

In about ten minutes I asked my son what he saw.

"I see Mom getting green."

"That's no hallucination," my wife said.

Five minutes later we all retired to our respective washrooms. This was the "trip" that everyone was talking about.

INFLATION IN THE NURSERY

The opening of the school year and the tight money situation are working hardships on many parents throughout the country.

My friend Block was in despair when I saw him the other day.

"When Roger was born," Block said, "we immediately took out an insurance policy for his education. Now because of inflation and the high cost of schooling, we've used it all up, and Roger still has six months to go."

"College is that expensive?" I asked.

"What do you mean, college?" Block said. "Roger goes to nursery school."

"Nursery school, huh?"

"Twenty-five hundred dollars a year, not counting the yearbook or the prom," Block said. "I guess our big mistake was sending Roger to prenursery school. You start a kid at three in school, and then you have no money left for his serious education when he becomes five. If I had to do it all over again, I would probably let him stay in his sandbox, but Alice was adamant about his getting a good, solid background."

"Couldn't you borrow some money from the bank to let Roger finish out nursery school?"

"Well, we did borrow a thousand dollars at the beginning of the summer."

"What happened to it?"

"We used it to send Roger to day camp."

"At least the money wasn't wasted," I said. "Aren't there any government grants for kids who want to finish out nursery school?"

"I looked into it. Most of the grants available are in graduate work for children who are either in the fifth grade or above. The particular nursery school that Roger goes to could have gotten a large grant from the government if it was willing to do research in germ warfare. But the headmistress said she wouldn't allow her children to do any research at the school that couldn't be published later."

"I guess scholarships are out?" I said.

"You don't understand," Block said. "It isn't just the tuition that kills you in nursery school. It's the school bus, finger paints, clay, and chocolate milk that really mounts up the cost. You have to add another fifteen hundred dollars for that."

"It's like a yacht," I said. "It isn't the initial cost but the upkeep that counts."

"Exactly. I went to Yale for what it's costing me to send Roger through nursery school. But when I tell him this, it doesn't seem to faze him at all. Kids take everything for granted these days."

"You haven't suggested to Roger he could wait on tables to earn part of the tuition himself?"

"Alice is against it. She says nursery school should be a happy time for a child, and a kid shouldn't have to worry about working just because his father hadn't made adequate plans for his education."

"You do seem to be on a spot," I admitted. "But I guess the day Roger graduates from nursery school, you'll realize all the sacrifice and agony were worthwhile."

"I probably would, but Roger has already indicated he wants to go on to first grade."

WHO'S WORRIED

One of the troubles with the world these days is that people have too much to worry about. You barely get over worrying about one thing, and you have to start worrying about something else.

Most Americans aren't equipped to worry about everything, and yet we constantly are told by scientists, politicians, generals, social workers, doctors, lawyers, TV commentators, newspaper editorial writers, and columnists that we'd better start worrying, or else.

My family thinks we have the solution to the problem. And since it's worked so well for us, I thought I'd pass it on to other people in hopes it might work for them. We decided a couple of weeks ago that each of us would worry about only one thing, to the exclusion of all other things.

For example, my father decided to worry only about the Middle East. Since he's been worried about the Middle East, none of the rest of us has to worry about it, and we're free to worry about the things that interest us.

My sister Alice worries about China for us. Anytime she

reads anything about Mao or the Red Guards, she'll call us up and say, "I'm very worried." Naturally, we're very relaxed about it because we always say to ourselves, "China's her problem."

My sister Edith worries about the population explosion. Why she decided on the population explosion we'll never know, except that one day she claimed she heard either on the *Johnny Carson Show*, the *Merv Griffin Show*, or the *Joey Bishop Show*—she can't remember which one—that by the year 2000 each person will have only twenty square inches of land to stand on. Now she skims through the papers, and if she doesn't find a population explosion story, she's free to enjoy the day.

We were fortunate in that my Uncle Oscar said he'd like to worry about Vietnam. No one really wanted to worry about Vietnam, since it takes up so much time, but Oscar said he'd rather worry about Vietnam than the riots in America's cities.

My sister Doris, who is a Francophobe, worries exclusively about Charles de Gaulle. She got into a fight with Edith, my population explosion sister, the other day because Edith said De Gaulle really wasn't worth worrying about. But Doris said she'd worry about what she darn pleased, and she's been very anxious ever since De Gaulle's trip to Canada.

My wife chose to worry about the cigarette-smoking scare. I tried to talk her out of it because the more she worries, the more cigarettes she smokes. But since she now does all the worrying for us about cigarettes, the rest of the family can continue to smoke without a care in the world.

My brothers-in-law also have chosen one subject each to worry about. Harold worries about auto safety, Arthur worries about air pollution, but the only thing we could get Iz to worry about was the Boston Red Sox.

Because I live in Washington, the family asked me to worry about President Johnson. At first I objected, since worrying about LBJ is a full-time job, and I wouldn't have any time to think about anything else. But they pointed out that since I've been worried about him for such a long time for myself, I could just as easily do it for them.

I agreed reluctantly, and while I haven't been sleeping very well since, at least I'm not worrying about Richard Nixon anymore. That's Aunt Molly's job.

2

✖ ✖ ✖ ✖ ✖ ✖ ✖ ✖ ✖ ✖ ✖ ✖ ✖ ✖ ✖

HOW TO WIN THE WAR

TEACHING CHINA A LESSON

Secretary of State Dean Rusk announced at his press conference that the real reason we are fighting in Vietnam is to contain Red China.

This came as good news to the Vietnamese people, many of whom are still not too sure what the war is all about.

Two Vietnamese peasants were huddled in a foxhole during a bombing raid.

"Say," said one of them to the other. "Did you hear the good news? This war has nothing to do with us. It's really between China and the United States."

"No kidding?" the other peasant said, hugging the earth as a bomb exploded. "Where did you hear that?"

"On the radio. You see, the reason why the United States is fighting in Vietnam is to contain China's expansionist ambitions. This is America's way of telling China to keep her hands off Southeast Asia."

Another bomb exploded.

"I wish there were another way of doing it," the peasant said.

"That's the trouble with you, Dao. You never can see the big picture. If the United States doesn't show that it's willing to honor its commitments in Vietnam, then every country in Southeast Asia will fall."

A bomb hit a hut about 100 feet from the foxhole.

"I guess I'm just selfish at heart," Dao said. "I really can't get too excited about what is happening in the rest of Southeast Asia at the moment."

"Dao, I'm surprised at you. There are one billion Chinese people, and they are committed to taking over one billion free people, and if it weren't for the United States bombing us, they would do it tomorrow."

Several fields caught on fire.

"Okay, I grant you that the free world has a great stake in Vietnam. But even so I don't enjoy being bombed."

"Nobody likes being bombed. But once you understand the reasons behind it, then it all makes sense."

"If this is really a contest between the United States and

China, why don't the Americans bomb China? Why don't the Americans bomb China instead of us?"

"Because that would get China into the war, and the United States doesn't want China in the war, stupid."

"Don't call me stupid. I don't see why we should be bombed just because the United States doesn't want to bomb China."

"Good grief, Dao, do you want to remain a peasant all your life? Secretary Rusk has spelled it out as clearly as possible. He's even willing to stop the bombing if Hanoi will go to the conference table."

"Why won't Hanoi go to the conference table?"

"Because if it does, the Chinese will lose face."

"I was afraid of that."

Another bomb exploded a few feet from the foxhole, and dirt fell on both men.

Dao said, "When did Rusk say the Chinese would see reason so he wouldn't have to bomb us anymore?"

"He said he wasn't sure, but possibly in the next generation."

BOMBING OVER CANADA

One of the most reassuring things that has happened recently is the Johnson Administration's confident reading of what is going on in the minds of the Red Chinese. The President has assured us that there are hardly any risks involved in bombing so close to the Red Chinese border, and we're told that Peking "knows" we have no intention of getting into a war with them at this time.

What has many people in Washington worried is not that the Red Chinese will become involved directly in the Vietnam conflict (we have Dean Rusk's pledge they won't), but that what the United States is doing in North Vietnam could start a precedent for future wars of liberation.

Suppose ten years from now President de Gaulle is "stalemated" in his efforts to free the French people of Canada from their despotic rulers in Ottawa. By this time he will have committed the French Army, the French Navy, and the French Foreign Legion to the war, yet Ottawa will have refused to give up. De Gaulle will be faced with a very tough decision.

"*Monsieur le Président*, we have no choice but to bomb Ottawa, Toronto, and Winnipeg. English-speaking Canada must be taught a lesson once and for all," a general says.

"But if we bomb Toronto, won't we run the risk of the United States getting in the war on the side of the Canadian aggressors?"

"*Mais non, Monsieur le Président.* If you go on the television and say that France does not desire a wider war with the United States, and all she is doing is trying to get Ottawa to come to the conference table, they will have no choice but to stay out of it."

"Ah, yes, but suppose the United States does not accept this and feels that her border is being threatened."

"Do not worry, *Monsieur le Président*. Our American experts say the United States is having so many riots in their country that they couldn't possibly get involved in a foreign engagement. This is the perfect time to escalate."

"All right, you may bomb, but only military targets. Perhaps the outskirts of the cities to start with."

Three days later De Gaulle is awakened in the middle of the night.

"*Monsieur le Président*, a squadron of *Mystères* got lost and bombed Minneapolis by mistake."

"I was afraid of that."

"Do not be worried. We notified Mexico to notify Washington that it was a mistake and that we apologize and will try not to do it again."

"That's good thinking, General. The Americans must know we have no quarrel with them. Has there been a reaction?"

"The President of the United States indicated he was very angry, but our intelligence informs us that they will not do anything but splutter."

At this point another phone rings. "*Monsieur le Président*, our radar reports that the United States has just launched missiles that are heading straight for the French coast."

"You mean they're attacking us just because we bombed Minneapolis by mistake? I thought you assured me the United States wouldn't get into the Canadian war under any circumstances."

"Ah, *Monsieur le Président*, one never knows what's going on in the minds of those wily Occidentals."

NO ATHEISTS IN FOXHOLES

Dispatches from South Vietnam report that the American GI's are getting sore about the political strife in the cities, and it's beginning to rub them that they have to do a lot of the fighting alone. There was a time in the Vietnam war when it was very rare for an American GI to see a Vietcong soldier. But this has all changed. The American GI has seen all the Vietcong he wants to, but it's very rare now for him to see a South Vietnamese soldier.

Two GI's were discussing this in the central highlands the other day.

"Remember the good old days," one of them said, "when we were their advisers?"

"That was before my time," the other one replied. "Frankly, I've never seen a South Vietnamese soldier. What do they look like?"

"It's been so long since I've seen them myself, but as I remember, they look like the Vietcong, except, of course, they have American uniforms."

"Charlie Baer was in Saigon sometime ago, and he said he saw some South Vietnamese soldiers. They were guarding General Ky's palace. He said they looked firstclass."

"I hear they're great at fighting Buddhists."

"I heard the ones at Hue were great at fighting General Ky's troops."

"There's nothing like having highly trained troops on your side."

"There's a rumor going around that the South Vietnamese troops might soon be sent out of the cities to fight the Vietcong."

"I heard that rumor before, but I doubt there's anything to it. If they pull out of the cities, who's going to guard the government?"

"Why couldn't we guard the government for a change and let the South Vietnamese fight the Vietcong?"

"That would be interfering in the affairs of another country, and we're not supposed to do that. But I did hear they're thinking of attaching a South Vietnamese soldier as an adviser with each American outfit just to keep up our morale."

"That would be nice," the other soldier said. "What would he do?"

"He could explain to us what we're doing out here."

"Do you think it would help much?"

"It might. Let's say they sent out one adviser. He would probably ask for an assistant, and then the assistant would ask for a jeep and driver, and the driver of the jeep would ask for a machine gunner, and before you know it, we'd have a lot of South Vietnamese soldiers in the field."

"Do you believe it would work?"

"How do you think we got here? We started out with twenty advisers in all of South Vietnam, and now we have four hundred thousand soldiers. It would be great if we could do the same thing to them."

"I understand that the South Vietnamese are very anxious for us to lick the Vietcong, and they'll support us in any way they can, short of widening the war."

"They say there are no atheists in foxholes in South Vietnam," his friend said.

"There are no Buddists either."

"Well, I guess we'd better get started again. President Johnson says we're not only fighting for the South Vietnamese, but we're fighting for free people everywhere."

"Where are the free people fighting?"

"Damned if I know. They must be around here somewhere."

HOW HIGH THE WAR?

Everyone knows the Viet war is costly, but no one realized how costly until the Washington Post revealed that it costs $332,000 to kill one Vietcong. The writer arrived at his figure by taking the monthly average of enemy killed and dividing it by the monthly cost of the war, which now seems to be running at a rate of $1.7 billion.

If these figures are correct, it would take $332,000,000 to kill 1,000 of the enemy, and even if we found a division of North Vietnamese soldiers, we wouldn't have the funds to destroy it.

It is obvious that if we want to have both guns and butter

in 1968, we're going to have to cut down the cost of knocking off the Vietcong.

Better brains than I have been working on the problem, and while no decision has been made, these are a few suggestions that the experts have come up with.

It has been proposed that instead of bombs, American planes drop new automobiles that have been called in for defects on the suburbs of Hanoi. Once enough cars have been dropped, the North Vietnamese would proceed to kill each other on their own highways (provided we don't destroy the highways). The main value of this plan, besides eliminating the enemy, is that it would solve the problem of what the United States should do with its unsafe cars.

Another project that is being given close study is to drop pamphlets on North Vietnamese and Vietcong zones offering anyone who deserts to our side a $25,000 home, free education for his children, color television, and a paid-up membership in the country club of his choice.

This would come to far less than $332,000 and would certainly be a great propaganda victory for our side.

If the Vietcong deserter preferred, we could give him a numbered bank account in Switzerland, so Ho Chi Minh would never find out about it.

Still another suggestion is that the United States build American-type factories all along the North-South Vietnam border. The smoke from the factories, with the help of a prevailing southeasterly wind, would pollute the air of North Vietnam, and the communists would slowly expire. It might take a little longer than other methods of eliminating the enemy, but the factories could be making war materials, so all the effort would not be wasted.

This is a little far-out and would require a great deal of coordination, but there are supposed to be quite a few American draft dodgers in Canada. In exchange for an amnesty, we would persuade them to go to Hanoi, and they could teach North Vietnamese students how to avoid their draft. If there were enough North Vietnamese draft dodgers who would refuse to fight, we could save several billion dollars a year.

No idea is too farfetched in time of war, and one that is also being considered has to do with giving out "contracts" to certain people in the American underworld. The going rate in the underworld to wipe out somebody is $25,000.

The idea would be for the United States to make a contract with an underworld syndicate and let private enterprise take over the elimination of our Vietcong friends.

These are only a few of the suggestions that are being considered. The reason why a solution to the problem has to be found fast is that at the present cost of fighting the enemy, we really can't afford to wipe them out. As a matter of fact, the fewer Vietcong we kill, the more money we save and the stronger our economy will be to fight the war.

HOW TO WIN THE WAR

The debate on Vietnam has been escalating along with the fighting, and now it's rare to go to a party and not get into a hot fight over what we should or should not be doing there.

Professor Heinrich Applebaum, the military analyst of *Seventeen* magazine, has just written a book titled *How to Fight the Vietnam War in the Living Room*. It is the only book written for both doves and hawks, and I was happy to interview him about it.

"This war will not be won in the rice paddies of the Mekong Delta, but rather in the salons and renovated basements of the American home," Applebaum told me.

"How does one start a discussion on the Vietnam war?"

"The best way is to say, 'I agree we shouldn't have been there in the first place, but—' It's a perfect opener if you're a hawk, and it shows you're willing to concede that the government has made mistakes."

"And if you're a dove?"

"Your opening line should be: 'I'm not for just pulling out and leaving South Vietnam in the lurch, but—' This should prove to your listeners that you're a man of reason, and you're not going to get emotional about the issue."

"As a hawk, what should you do next?"

"Mention Munich, the domino theory, and our commitment to the free world, not necessarily in that order."

"And if you're a dove?"

"Talk about the stupidity of the French, the naiveté of John Foster Dulles, and the right for people to have their own revolutions without outside interference from the United States."

"How do you follow it up?"

"You have to quote sources. If you're a hawk, you quote Joe Alsop, Bob Hope, Cardinal Spellman, Barry Goldwater, and *Time* Magazine. If you're a dove, you refer to Walter Lippmann's last column, speeches by Senator Fulbright and Robert F. Kennedy, and testimony by General Gavin, Robert Lowell, and Joan Baez. Even if they didn't say something, you can always claim they did. No one in the living room is going to be able to check up on you."

"Don't you quote President Johnson, Secretary Dean Rusk, or Robert McNamara?"

"It's hardly worth it. Neither the hawks nor the doves believe anything the people in our government tell them."

"Outsiders always know more," I agreed.

"Now if you see the argument is running down, you can always refer to a book you read on Vietnam. People are very impressed with anyone in the crowd who has read a book, and it shows you've gone deeper into the subject than anyone else in the room."

"Any special book?"

"The best one is a title that no one has ever heard of, particularly if it's been written by someone with a foreign name. It will make the other side very mad, and he'll have to come up with a book of his own."

"It gets harder as you go along," I said.

"The important thing is to speak with authority and pretend to know what you're talking about."

"But suppose you lose the argument?"

"You can always punch the guy in the nose."

KEEPING UP MORALE

In all the discussions of the bombing of North Vietnam, the one word that keeps popping up is "morale." Secretary McNamara stated in Congressional testimony that while the bombing did not stop the infiltration from North Vietnam, it has been a major factor in keeping up morale in South Vietnam.

Visitors coming back from Hanoi and North Vietnam say that the American bombing of North Vietnam has had a tremendous effect on North Vietnamese morale and that it has given the North the will and strength to go on.

So here you have one of the most ticklish situations of the Vietnam war. Whose morale would be hurt most if you stopped bombing North Vietnam?

If it's true that the bombing of North Vietnam by American planes has helped North Vietnamese morale to the point that they are determined to continue the war, then the obvious answer is that we should stop the bombing. Without American planes overhead, Communist morale could fall apart, and Hanoi might make a dash to the peace table.

The only thing wrong with this is that if we stopped the bombing of North Vietnam, we might do untold damage to morale in South Vietnam. It is no secret that the Americans have been bombing South Vietnam more than they have North Vietnam, mainly because there is more to bomb in the South. The South Vietnamese are willing to put up with this as long as they know that North Vietnam is getting its share of bombs.

To stop bombing North Vietnam would mean that there would be a lot more planes available to bomb South Vietnam, which certainly isn't anything the South Vietnamese are looking forward to.

Then there is the question of U.S. morale to be considered. If American flyers were forbidden to bomb North Vietnam and were allowed to bomb only South Vietnam, their morale would go down 100 percent. You can always make a mistake bombing a target in South Vietnam, but anything you hit in North Vietnam is considered fair game.

The final factor to be taken into consideration is morale on the American home front. Every time there is a pause in the bombing on North Vietnam, a large proportion of the American people get very depressed, and Congressmen and Senators start making speeches saying we are not backing up our boys at the front.

As soon as we resume the bombing, morale at home zooms, and everyone is happy again because we're proving Communist aggression doesn't pay.

I haven't mentioned what the American bombing of North Vietnam is doing to the Red Chinese morale, but from all reports they would like to see us continue bombing the North just so Hanoi won't start peace negotiations.

The Soviet Union, which we've been trying to woo over to our side in the past year or so, is having its own morale problem because its ground-to-air missiles haven't been working too well in North Vietnam.

So when you get right down to it, the big issue of Vietnam boils down to morale, and if we can solve that one, we can end the war.

MILITARY TARGETS ONLY

When it was decided to bomb inside the city limits of Haiphong, the Pentagon went to great lengths to explain the operation. The Defense Department said it was bombing only a power plant in the city and that very few houses had been damaged in the raid.

I went over to see my friend at the Pentagon to find out what *really* was going on, and I found him studying a street map of Haiphong. He didn't deny that the bombing had taken place, but he did deny that the bombing was an escalation of the war.

"Our plan is to bomb only military targets in the city," he assured me.

"What are you doing with the map?"

"My job is to find military targets in Haiphong. For example, I notice that there are three Army-Navy surplus stores located here on Won Ton Street. They might be worth bombing, except for the fact that Won Ton Street bisects the Fourth of June Boulevard, where they have a maternity shop. It could be very dicey if we hit the maternity shop by mistake."

"That's pretty tricky bombing," I said.

"Now over here on Ho-Ho Road is a gas station that should be knocked out, but it's only four blocks from the center of town. Since we don't want world opinion to go against us, we've decided not to bomb anything within a twenty-two-block radius of the Loew's Haiphong."

"That's a good idea," I said. "No one's going to criticize you if you bomb that far away from the Loew's Haiphong."

"I'm not so sure. The peaceniks are liable to grab at any straw."

"What's that red target you have circled?"

"That's a combination police station and fire department on lots of Lenin Street. We'd like to knock out the police station part of it, but we don't want to hurt the fire department, particularly since we're dropping incendiary bombs."

"I see you've got Phe Phi Phong Lane marked up."

"Yes, that's a condemned apartment house. The CIA says they're going to tear it down next week, so we thought we would save them a lot of time."

"You people are all heart," I said. "Are there any other military targets you've got marked down?"

"Well, over there on Yum Yum Tree Street is the Mao Tse-tung Red Guard Chewing Gum Factory."

"Is that a military target?"

"Of course, it is. The chewing gum is being used by the North Vietnamese to repair the struts on their airplanes. We knock out the chewing gum factory, and we knock out their air potential."

"Then by all means knock it out," I urged.

"Now here is the high-rent district, and it's giving us terrible problems. It is mostly residential, but over here is the Behn Ho-Gun Golf Course, and we understand that underneath it is a complex of tunnels with all sorts of tanks, guns, and mortars. We'd like to bomb it, but we're afraid we'd get all the golf fans in American upset at us for wrecking the links."

"Not to mention the putting greens," I added.

"Exactly. So in deference to the golf buffs in this country, we've marked the Behn Ho-Gun off limits, at least for the time being."

"I don't see how they can accuse you of escalation when you're not even bombing their golf courses."

Just then an assistant brought in another map.

"What's that?" I asked.

"It's a street map of Hanoi."

"I was afraid of that," I said.

"Don't worry. We're just going to hit the military targets."

BRIDGING THE GAP

Representative Thomas M. Rees (D. Calif.) raised a question in a newsletter that has been bothering many people: How many bridges does North Vietnam really have?

He says that despite continuous bombing of bridges, the Ho government seems to be building them much faster than we can destroy them. In a two-week period, a military spokesman announced, we had destroyed 133 bridges, a very impressive figure.

But what has Congressman Rees worried is that during the same period the United States military announced that infiltration into South Vietnam had increased. It seems that the more targets we knock out in North Vietnam, the more troops are sent into South Vietnam.

Rees raises these questions: Are the North Vietnamese winning the race for spans? And is the United States suffering from a bridge gap?

To find the answer to these questions, I interviewed the Undersecretary of Defense in charge of destroying bridges. He had a simple explanation for the whole thing.

"You must remember," he said, "when we started bombing North Vietnam, we expected Hanoi to cave in immediately. Therefore, there was no effort made to ration the country's military targets over any period of time. The bombers went in there and destroyed everything without thought to the future.

"Much to everyone's surprise, the bombing did not have the effect we wanted. Instead of giving in, North Vietnamese resistance stiffened, and suddenly the United States found itself with a shortage of bombing targets."

"To paraphrase Churchill," I said, "never had so much been done by so few so fast."

"Something like that," the Undersecretary said. "Well we were caught flatfooted, so we asked the Administration to declare a temporary bombing cessation.

"They could announce the reason we were doing it was to give Hanoi a chance to seek peace negotiations, but in fact, the pause would give the North Vietnamese a chance to repair their bridges, so we would have some targets to bomb again."

"It was clever strategy," I admitted.

"Unfortunately, our bombing was so good that as soon as we were permitted to fly over North Vietnam again, we destroyed all the bridges that had been repaired. This left us in a helluva predicament, so we decided to go after their old storage tanks and railroad yards. But once again we knocked them out in a few raids, and the realization started to dawn on us that the larger the raids, the fewer results we had to show for it. In the beginning the destruction of an oil-storage-tank farm was a big event, but as time went on, we found ourselves happy to announce that one hundred and fifty B-52's had knocked out two jeeps and eight water buffaloes."

"I remember that," I said.

"So we decided the only solution to the problem was to drop our own bridges on North Vietnam and then destroy them. The first wave of bombers would let go with the bridges, and the second wave would come on a half hour later and bomb them. In this way, we could truthfully say we had knocked out more bridges than the North Vietnamese had to start with."

"And it's working?" I asked.

"I should hope to tell you, it's working. We've got the Communists completely confused because they can't account for the bridges we've destroyed. And it's also played havoc with North Vietnamese morale. The soldiers there are very embittered. They want to know why if North Vietnam has that many bridges, they have to swim across so many dirty rivers all the time."

KNOW YOUR ENEMY

"Do you know what one of the troubles with the Vietnam war is?" a colonel in the Pentagon asked me recently.

"I'm sure I don't," I said in all honesty.

"We can't make an enemy out of the enemy."

I thought about this for a few minutes, and then I said, "How's that again?"

"Just what I said. It's impossible to describe the enemy in terms that will get to the American people emotionally."

"You mean we can't call them yellow bellies as we did the Japanese in World War II," I said.

"Exactly. Nor can we refer to them in racial terms, because the people on our side look exactly the same as the people on *their* side."

"I never thought about that," I said.

"The problem is: How do you portray the Vietcong in photographs and movies for what they really are without offending the South Vietnamese at the same time?"

"Through atrocities, of course," I replied. "Can't you show the Vietcong committing atrocities agains the South Vietnamese people?"

"It's awfully difficult," he said, "because our television cameramen and still photographers take pictures only of the atrocities we commit, but never get any shots of the ones the Cong commit."

"The solution then would be to get our cameramen attached to the Vietcong," I said.

"It's a good suggestion," the colonel said, "but every time we ask Hanoi if we can have our camera crews cover their operations, they say we can't until we stop the bombing."

"And we can't stop the bombing," I said.

"Of course not. At least not until they stop raping and pillaging the South Vietnamese villages."

"Which nobody will believe they're doing because we have no pictures?"

"That's the difficulty. We don't even have any good films of the North Vietnamese in Hanoi calling for the raping and pillaging of South Vietnam. Remember, in World War II, those wonderful shots of Hitler, Goebbels, and Goering screaming oaths at the Allies?"

"How could anyone forget?"

"And those pictures of Tojo in Tokyo?" he said.

"They were worth thousands of words."

"Well, we haven't been able to get any shots of Ho Chi Minh that show him looking like anything except a starving Santa Claus."

"You can't get the people riled up about that," I admitted. "Isn't it possible to make the Vietcong wear uniforms so we can tell them apart from the good guys?"

"That's another problem we have. The Vietcong don't wear uniforms. They look just like everybody else in Vietnam."

"Why don't we send a bombing mission over the Vietcong areas and drop World War II Nazi uniforms on them? You can't help hating someone in a Nazi uniform."

"We've thought about it, but the Vietcong are too small. The uniforms would never fit them, and they'd probably use the helmets for bathtubs."

"Well, at least it taught us a lesson."

"What's that?"

"We should never get into a war where people on both sides look alike."

THE CREDIBILITY GAP

There is much talk about the credibility gap in regard to the Vietnam war. Dispatches from Saigon indicate the Pentagon is trying, as usual, to manage the news. This is understandable and even defensible on military grounds. But what is dangerous is that the planting of stories in Saigon by the Defense Department is causing a credibility gap in the Pentagon itself.

This is how it works.

A top-secret directive from the Pentagon to Saigon briefing officers instructs them to announce that Air Force raids on North Vietnam have knocked out 90 percent of all enemy fuel capacity, and there is no chance of the North Vietnamese supplying their troops in the South.

A story based on the official announcement is filed by the correspondents in Saigon to their newspapers back home. The Washington *Post* prints the story the next morning, and it is read by everyone, including Colonel Zilch, who works in the Pentagon on planning and organization.

Colonel Zilch, unaware that the Pentagon has planted the story to keep up South Vietnamese morale, calls a meeting of his staff and informs them that on the basis of the latest reports there is no need to send any more American troops or supplies to Vietnam.

A staff member points out that his reports indicate only 50 percent of the oil depots were knocked out, and rather than the infiltration's being decreased, it has increased since the bombing.

Zilch replies that the reports are a few days old and then cites the Washington *Post* story out of Saigon as a much later and more up-to-date report, particularly since it was released by officials in Saigon who should know. Besides, Zilch points out, *The New York Times* confirmed the story.

The staff agrees that some action should be taken, and a paper is prepared recommending the calling off of troop shipments and cutting down the size of the draft.

This report goes to a general who assumes the staff report is based on latest intelligence estimates of the situation and informs the Joint Chiefs of Staff who advise the Administration that the war is going well and 90 percent of all the oil in North Vietnam has been destroyed.

A high Administration official in the White House tells the President, "I was suspicious of the story when I read it in the newspapers, but now that it's been confirmed by the Pentagon, it must be true." The high Administration official then holds a background-not-for-attribution news conference, in which he informs newspapermen that we are winning the war in Vietnam, and no more American troops will be needed.

The newspapermen write the story quoting "high Government officials," and when the story appears in the Saigon *Post*, the staff officers out there have fits. They demand an explanation from the Pentagon. The Pentagon, realizing what probably happened, tells the briefing officers in Saigon to inform the press that a new estimate of the situation shows we knocked out only 20 percent of the oil dumps and that the infiltration rate from the North has increased as a result of the bombings.

The briefing was held in Saigon, the stories are filed, and the next morning over his breakfast, Colonel Zilch reads the news.

He is horrified at the switch in figures and has his staff draw up a paper recommending the immediate shipment of additional troops and the doubling of supplies.

This time the general who receives the paper fails to forward it to the Joint Chiefs of Staff. "If Zilch was wrong yesterday," he tells his aide, "he's probably wrong today, too."

"Are you going to ask him to resign?" the aide asks.

"No, but cancel his subscription to the Washington *Post*."

BUT WHAT IF THEY ACCEPT?

The Manila Summit Conference attended by President Johnson and Southeast Asia heads of state was successful beyond anybody's wildest dreams. The final communiqué, announcing that the United States and other troops fighting on the South Vietnamese side would pull out within six months, provided Hanoi did the same, was a masterful touch of diplomacy.

There is only one thing that could mar the success of the

conference—and that is if the North Vietnamese accepted the proposal.

I would hate to think what would happen in the State Department if word were received that the North Vietnamese had accepted the terms of the Manila Conference and were ready to begin pulling out Communist troops immediately.

"Sir, we've just received word that Hanoi is willing to negotiate a peace settlement according to guidelines set down in Manila."

"They wouldn't dare."

"It's true. It's been confirmed by our embassies in Moscow, Paris, and Dar es Salaam."

"The dirty Commie double crossers. They knew that proposal was just for world consumption. Get me Hardright in here immediately."

"Yes, sir. By the way, the Pentagon is calling frantically. I guess they must have heard the news also."

"Stall 'em till we find a solution to this problem."

Hardright comes in.

The Deputy Secretary glares at him. "Hardright, this latest peace proposal was your idea. How do you explain the fact that Hanoi accepted it?"

"I can't understand it, sir. It went along with all the lines of the other peace feelers that they had rejected in the past. We put in enough clinkers to make it entirely unacceptable to them. You know what I think, sir. They're up to something."

"You're darned right they're up to something. If we pull out all our troops in six months, and they pull out all their troops in six months, there will be nobody left in South Vietnam but the Ky government and the Vietcong. You know and I know the Ky government isn't strong enough to fight off the Vietcong."

"Can I help it if the North Vietnamese are no longer intractable?"

"I'm not blaming you, Hardright, but we've got to find a solution to this problem, or we'll be back where we started in 1956."

"Why don't we announce that their acceptance of our proposal is unacceptable to us on the grounds that in deciding to accept our peace plan, they have shown bad faith."

"I'm afraid that wouldn't make us look very good in the eyes of the world. If they accept the peace plan, we will have no choice but to go ahead with our end of the bargain."

"I knew it was a mistake for President Johnson to go to Manila," Hardright cried.

"I have one idea that I've been kicking around in my head. Suppose Hanoi pulls all its troops back to the North and we pull all our troops out from the South? The South Vietnamese Army would be in charge of keeping the peace in the country."

"They would never be able to do it," Hardright said.

"They might," the Deputy Secretary said, "if we sent in a few American military advisers."

"By golly," Hardright said, "what a great idea! We could announce that the advisers are only being sent in so the South Vietnamese could help themselves."

"Exactly. Our people would be used only to train their troops."

"How many military advisers do you think we should send in for a start?"

"Let's just send in five hundred. We can always add to that if the situation gets out of hand."

NOTHING TO FEAR

There has been growing fear in Washington of late that the Johnson Administration is escalating its efforts to cut off all criticism of the way the President and his people are handling the Vietnam war.

This fear, of course, is groundless because President Johnson has said many times that this is a free country and he not only welcomes dissent, but seeks it out.

He has also said, though, that the dissenters are prolonging the war, and the more his critics scream for peace, the more encouraged Hanoi is to continue the fighting.

Therefore, the burden of ending the war is not on the Administration anymore, but on the critics. And in a free society it is a tough burden to carry.

I found my friend Polanski, who has been a critic of the war for some time, muttering to himself the other day.

"Let's see," he said. "If I'm against the war, and I say I'm against the war, that means the war will continue. But if I say I'm for the war, even if I'm against it, that means it will end."

"That's right, Polanski," I said. "If you would just shut up, Hanoi would come to the conference table in twenty-four hours."

"But I don't like the way the war is going," he protested.

"No one likes the way the war is going, Polanski, but the more you say you don't like the way the war is going, the worse the war gets. At least that's what President Johnson says."

"But if I don't say I don't like the way the war is going, how will President Johnson know I don't like it?"

"President Johnson knows already that you don't like the way the war is going."

"Who told him?"

"Probably the FBI. But the important thing is he doesn't care if he knows it. What worries him is that Ho Chi Minh knows it."

"How would Ho Chi Minh know it?" Polanski wanted to know.

"Because President Johnson keeps talking about his U.S. critics' helping Ho Chi Minh all the time."

"But if I shut up, then President Johnson will think I'm for everything he's doing over there."

"I don't think that would bother President Johnson too much."

"But it would bother me. After all, if we don't have any dissent in this country, then we're no better than the Communists."

"Now that's ridiculous, Polanski. There will always be healthy dissent in this country. Why you could get up tomorrow and attack Lady Bird's beautification program and you wouldn't hear a peep from the White House. You could also attack Senators Fulbright, Kennedy, McGovern, and Church, and even though they're of the President's own political party, he would welcome your criticism. That's the kind of man the President is."

"Isn't there any way of telling President Johnson I don't approve of his policies without Hanoi finding out about it?" Polanski asked.

"It's not easy, Polanski, particularly when you're wearing that sweat shirt which says MAKE LOVE NOT WAR."

"Okay, you've persuaded me. I'll make a new sweat shirt."

Polanski took out a brush and paint. As I looked over his shoulder, he painted on his sweat shirt BOMB HANOI BACK TO THE STONE AGE.

"That's wonderful, Polanski," I said. "You may even win the Nobel Peace Prize for that one."

3

❌❌❌❌❌❌❌❌❌❌❌❌❌❌❌

THE FATHER OF THE BUG

"WHAT HATH THE NRA WROUGHT?"

The National Rifle Association has not only been fighting against any decent federal gun legislation, but in the latest issue of its magazine, the NRA recommends that citizens arm themselves and join posses and unorganized militia to protect American communities against riots. The NRA editorial goes on to say that the police cannot do the job, and it's essential that everyone buy a gun.

As soon as I read the editorial, I rushed down to my friendly local gunshop and told the clerk, "Give me a .22 pistol, so I can protect myself against the forces of evil that are running rife in this country."

"Yes, sir." The clerk smiled. "I see you read the NRA editorial."

"You're darned tootin'," I said. "And as a good American, I want a gun at my side at all times."

While the clerk was looking for the gun, a man in dirty blue denims came in and shouted to another clerk, "Hey, baby, I want to get my hands on a nice snub-nosed .32 revolver."

"Say, wait a minute," I said nervously. "You people aren't supposed to be buying guns."

"That's how much you know, man. I just read this crazy editorial in the National Rifle Association magazine, and it said if I ain't satisfied with *my* police protection, I should go out and arm myself. Well, that's what I'm doing, baby."

My clerk came back with the .22 revolver. "On second thought," I said, "I think I better look at your .38 Colts. This .22 looks too small for me."

The man in the denims watched me closely and then shouted to his clerk: "Hey, baby, you better forget that .32. I'll look at a .45 pistol instead."

As I inspected the .38, I whispered to my clerk, "You don't have a German Luger for sale, do you?"

The clerk disappeared to look for a Luger, and I said to the man, "You know I'm only buying my gun for self-defense."

"That's all I'm buying mine for, baby. A man's got to protect his life and home. It's in the Constitution. Man starts

50

shooting at me, I'll start shooting back. You buying a Luger, man?"

"I'm just looking at it," I said.

"Hey, daddio," he said to the clerk, "I think I'd rather have a shotgun."

The man stared at me. "You going for a shotgun, baby?"

"I'm not sure," I said. "Unfortunately, the NRA didn't say what kind of gun to buy. I guess a shotgun is as good as anything if you don't trust your local police force."

"Maybe so, but I like a gun with more firepower. You don't want to have to stop to load and reload when someone's shooting at you all the time." His clerk brought out a .30-30 Springfield.

"No, man. That won't do. You got something in the automatic line? Maybe a carbine?"

My hands were perspiring. I said to my clerk, "On second thought instead of a shotgun, I'd like to see your small lightweight submachine guns."

The man looked at the carbine a few minutes. "I don't think it will do the job. You have any 20-millimeter cannons?"

"Never mind the submachine gun," I shouted to the clerk. "Let me see what you got in bazookas!"

The other man in the store asked for a flame thrower, and when the clerk said he didn't have any, he paid for his 20-millimeter cannon.

I had my bazooka gift-wrapped.

"I'll see you around, baby," the man smiled maliciously as he put the cannon over his shoulder.

"Yeah," I said, stuffing my bazooka shells in a shopping bag. "I'll see you around."

A SAD POLICY

People who are perplexed about State Department foreign policy will be happy to hear there is one. It isn't much of a policy; but at least it's ours, and I can now reveal what it is.

It is based on waiting for people to die. Since we can't very well do anything with many of the present world rulers, our only hope is that they will soon take a trip to that Great Big United Nations in the Sky.

I was fortunate to speak to the Assistant Secretary of State for Funereal Affairs, whose department is working on the policy. As I entered his large, quiet, dignified office, I heard organ music in the background. The Secretary was wearing a mourning coat, a gray tie, striped pants, and a somber, almost sad expression on his face.

"Are you the bereaved?" he asked.

"No," I said. "I'm a newspaperman, and I wanted to talk to you about our foreign policy. Is it true that it's based on waiting for leaders of different countries to die?"

"We don't refer to them as leaders," he said quietly, "but as the loved ones. Please don't get us wrong. The State Department does not want anyone to die, but if certain rulers would expire, all our problems would be solved."

"Who are some of the leaders you're waiting for to pass away?"

"I'd rather not mention any names. But there are certain people giving us tremendous amounts of trouble. It is our belief that if they were no longer with us, we could then proceed with policies favorable to the United States."

"Do you have any of these policies on hand?"

"Yes, we do. Please follow me." He took me into a large, softly lighted room where all the different State Department policies were on display.

"This is our most inexpensive model," he said. "You will notice that although it has no frills, it is very solid and will hold up in any kind of weather. We use this for our smaller countries in Africa and South America. It costs only twenty-five million dollars.

"Over here is our medium-priced model. You will note this one is much more elaborate and has a pure velvet lining in it. It is perfectly suited for a European nation and can even be used behind the Iron Curtain, provided the mourners request it."

"How much does one of these cost?"

"Between fifty and one hundred million dollars, but that includes everything."

"What are those Oriental policies over there?"

"Ah, at the moment those are our most expensive models. If the right person dies, it might cost as much as a half billion dollars. But it is the most complete of all our policies and provides aid to the bereaved in every possible form from the cradle to the grave."

I looked over and saw a magnificent model, handcarved in mahogany and ivory.

"That looks like a French model," I said. "But it's very long, almost seven feet."

The Assistant Secretary of State blushed. "You weren't supposed to see that one. It's already been reserved."

I went back into his office, and he said, "You must understand we are not in any position to rush anybody. But the State Department is always prepared for that eventful day when one of our loved ones must leave us. Then and only then can we go ahead and bring solace to a saddened world. This has been our policy for years."

BABY FACE—A REMAKE

Ever since the Supreme Court rulings concerning the protection of a defendant's constitutional rights at the time of his arrest, the motion-picture people have been in a dither. Almost every gangster movie of the last forty years is now outdated and will have to be remade with the rights of the defendant kept in mind.

This is probably what the remake of *Baby Face Nelson* will look like. Baby Face has been betrayed by his jealous girl friend, and the cops have his farm hideout surrounded. The chief of police says over his loudspeaker, "Now hear this, Baby Face. The farmhouse is surrounded, and you don't have a chance. Come out with your hands up."

"Drop dead, copper," Baby Face shouts from the window, firing a shot at the same time.

"I must warn you, Baby Face," the chief says, "that anything you say will be held against you."

Baby Face lets go with a burst of a machine gun. "I don't intend to be taken alive, you dirty finks."

The chief ducks behind his car. Kneeling, he says, "Baby Face, I have to advise you that you have a choice of your own lawyer or we will provide you with a public defender, and you do not have to say anything to us when you come out of the farmhouse with your hands up, if you do not want to."

"I got lots to say," Baby Face shouts from the window. "Ha, ha, ha."

He lets go with another burst from the machine gun.

"If you're going to talk to us, Baby Face, you'll have to sign a waiver that no one made you say anything against your will."

"I'm signing nothing, copper. I know my rights. Like the case of *Gonzales vs. the State of Oklahoma,* no one can lay a finger on me until I'm brought before a magistrate and given a hot meal and a bubble bath."

"Now listen carefully, Baby Face," the police chief says. "We know you've killed twelve bank tellers and robbed six post offices, but constitutionally you have nothing to fear. Even if we can prove our case, you can always appeal on the grounds that because of this gunfight, you received adverse publicity in the newspapers and could not get a fair trial."

Baby Face fires another burst from his machine gun. "That's what you say now. I haven't forgotten what happened in the *Glutz vs. the People of Peoria, Illinois,* case when the coppers tricked Glutz into a confession by giving him two tickets to the Green Bay Packers–Baltimore Colts football game."

"The Third Circuit Court threw out the Glutz conviction, Baby Face," the chief shouts over the loudspeaker. "Didn't you read about the Third Circuit Court of Appeals ruling in *Nashville vs. Virginia Woolf?*"

"I haven't seen the newspapers lately," Baby Face shouts. "I've been holed up here, and if you want me, you're going to have to come and get me." *Rat-a-tat-tat.*

"Okay, Baby Face, have it your way, but don't say we're violating your constitutional rights."

The chief gives the signal to charge, and a hailstorm of lead fills the air. When the smoke clears, Baby Face is lying mortally wounded.

His mother rushes up to him and puts his head in her lap.

"They got me, Ma. Tell Melvin Belli the cops cheated him out of a fee," Baby Face gasps.

"Don't talk, son. If the police doctor doesn't patch you up, we can sue him for malpractice."

"But how, Ma?"

"Don't you remember, son, *Dillinger vs. the People of Malibu Beach, California?*"

THE FATHER OF THE BUG

Just when things were getting dull in Washington, Robert Kennedy, former Attorney General, and J. Edgar Hoover, head of the FBI, plunged headlong into a bitter brouhaha over who gave permission to bug certain elements of our society while violating their constitutional rights.

It is not general knowledge, but the bugging of telephones has been going on in the United States for almost a hundred years.

The first known case of the government bugging someone took place on March 10, 1876, in the laboratories of Alexander Graham Bell in Boston, Massachusetts. Mr. Bell had been working for some time on a new speaking device, which he called the telephone. In the next room was his assistant, Tom Watson. One day Bell said into his mouthpiece, "Watson, come here, I want you."

Watson rushed into the next room, threw his arms around Bell, and the telephone was born.

But unbeknownst to both Watson and Bell, a third person was listening in on their conversation. It was a young government investigator named J. E. Hoover, who was out to make a name for himself in the Justice Department.

J. E. took the next train for Washington. Breathlessly, he rushed in to see President Grant's Attorney General, who happened to be a man named Edwards Pierrepont. In the presence of department officials he played the primitive, crackling tape for them.

Attorney General Pierrepont couldn't believe his ears. "What hath God wrought?" he said.

J. E. said, "You have heard a tape of the first conversation ever bugged on a telephone."

"What the hell's a telephone?" the Attorney General wanted to know.

"It's a new invention by some Scotsman named Alexander Graham Bell. He wasn't a citizen, so I was very curious about what he was up to. I think 'Watson, come here, I want you,' is some sort of code, but I haven't had time to break it down yet."

"But what good is bugging a telephone?" the Attorney General demanded.

"I'd rather put it another way, sir. What good is a telephone if it isn't bugged? Don't you see what this invention means? If there are going to be telephones, we can listen in on them, and we can catch spies and crooks and Communists and bookies and juvenile delinquents and even lawyers."

"I don't know, J. E. The whole thing smells unconstitutional to me," the Attorney General said.

"But how else are we going to get the rats if we don't bug them on the telephone?" J. E. demanded.

"I'm the Attorney General of the United States, J. E., and I can't condone wiretapping of any kind unless it's in the national interest. On the other hand, if I didn't know about it, then I wouldn't be condoning it, would I?"

"Exactly my thoughts, sir. Just sign this letter saying you don't know anything about my tapping telephones, and it will be all the authority I need."

Little did Edwards Pierrepont know when he signed the letter that every other Attorney General after him would sign a similar letter until this year, when the Supreme Court wanted to know what was going on.

Alexander Graham Bell may have invented the telephone, but it was young J. E. Hoover who really made the invention pay off for law-abiding Americans everywhere.

POLLS APART

Sometime ago George Gallup's poll revealed that Senator Robert Kennedy was more popular than President Lyndon Baines Johnson. This obviously has caused some consternation at the White House, where polls play such an important part in the life of the Great Society.

I would have hated to have been the White House aide who had to break the news to the President about the results of the Gallup Poll. It must have gone something like this.

"Well, Marvin, read me some polls this morning, while I'm shaving."

"Yes, sir, Mr. President. The Lurleen Poll in Alabama says you're running eight percentage points ahead of Adam Clayton Powell."

"That's fine. What else have you got?"

"There's good news from the Lou Harris Survey in Southeast Asia. It reveals more people want you to bomb North Vietnam than they do Cambodia."

"What else, Marvin?"

"Elmo Roper has an excellent one, sir. He took a survey in Alaska, and more people up there recognized your name than they did either George Romney or Sonny Liston."

"Remind me to go up to Alaska one of these weekends, Marvin."

"You made the Ten Best-Dressed Men of the Year Poll again, Mr. President."

"Not many votes in that."

"Here's one from South America I think you'll be interested in. The Sombrero Organization of Public Opinion took a survey in Venezuela, and sixty-three percent of the people questioned said they'd rather listen to you on the Voice of America than either President Sukarno or Gamal Nasser."

"Remind me to send Hubert Humphrey to Venezuela one of these days."

"Oscar Quayle has been working the state of Montana for a couple of months, sir, and I must say he's come up with some heady stuff. You're more popular up there than either Jimmy Hoffa or the Atlanta Braves baseball team."

"I'll work in something nice about Montana at my next press conference. Is that all you've got?"

"The *Wall Street Journal* took a poll among its readers, and you're running fourteen percentage points ahead of Ralph Nader, George Meany, Arthur Schlesinger, and Norman Thomas."

"That's a fine newspaper."

"The Nielsen ratings have just come in, and Luci Baines' wedding had a higher rating than *Naked City, Queen for a Day,* and *My Mother the Car.*"

"Remind me to send an autographed picture to Mr. Nielsen. Say, isn't this the morning that the Gallup Poll comes out?"

"Yes, sir, it is."

"Well, what are you waiting for? Let's have it."

"It's a popularity survey. I don't think you'd be interested in it, Mr. President."

"Let's hear it, Marvin."

"It seems, for some reason I'll never understand, Gallup asked people whom they'd prefer in 1968 as President, and more people mentioned Bobby Kennedy than they did you. I'm sorry, sir."

"Nothing to be sorry about, Marvin. I never put much truck in polls anyway. They're bound to be wrong every time."

NO PEACE IN WASHINGTON

The big question everyone in the nation's capital is asking is, "Can there ever be peace in *Washington?*" As every day passes, the positions of President Johnson and Senator Kennedy harden, and the chances of a peaceful solution to the war in the Democratic Party grow dimmer and dimmer.

From his government-in-exile headquarters at Hickory Hill, Virginia, Senator Kennedy told a Japanese newspaperman he's willing to sit down with the President anywhere, at any time, provided the President stops bombing the press with news releases just when Kennedy is making a speech on the floor of the Senate.

A White House spokesman said that it still hopes to go to the conference table with the Kennedys, but first they must make some gesture to show they really want peace.

When asked what kind of gesture was expected of the Kennedys, the spokesman replied, "They have to stop infiltrating Arthur Schlesinger, Richard Goodwin, and John Kenneth Galbraith into *The New York Times,* the *Saturday Evening Post,* and the *Today* show."

When asked if they would consider a pause in the bombing of the Kennedys to see what the reaction would be, the White House spokesman replied, "We have tried a pause in the bombing, but it didn't do any good. Bobby Kennedy went off to Europe and escalated his attacks by meeting with President de Gaulle. We can't stand by and let the Great Society be shot in the back."

A Kennedy spokesman said he doubted the sincerity of the Johnson Administration in seeking to achieve a just and lasting peace in the Democratic Party. He said that on the one occasion when the President put out peace feelers to Bobby at the White House, the President spent two hours chewing out the Senator from New York. "Then the White House leaked the confrontation to the press, causing Bobby to lose face in front of his brother, Teddy. The Johnson Administration talks peace, but it continues to escalate the war."

When informed of what the Kennedy spokesman had said, the White House replied, "The Johnson Administration didn't seek out a war with the Kennedys, but it can't flinch from its responsibilities to the party. If it loses to the Kennedys, New York could fall, then California, and on the basis of the domino theory, every state could follow, and the whole country could be taken over by the Republicans. We owe it to the people never to let this country fall under Republican domination."

The White House spokesman continued that criticism of President Johnson by those supporting Senator Kennedy's speeches was just prolonging the war in the Democratic Party. "Senator Kennedy interprets any opposition of President Johnson as a sign that the country is divided and weak. If the critics did not publicly side with Kennedy, hostilities would cease overnight."

At Hickory Hill, Virginia, everyone scoffed at the White House statement. One of the Kennedy children said, "They call that a peace feeler? We've had better peace feelers from *Look* magazine."

In the meantime, neutral sources were working behind the scenes to find some way out of the impasse. One proposal for a truce was that President Johnson *not* go on television the same day Senator Kennedy gave an important foreign policy speech.

In exchange, Senator Kennedy would have to promise not to meet with Pope Paul VI the same day President Johnson gave a press conference.

President Johnson has told intimates he would do anything to achieve peace in the Democratic Party. He said, "Ah'd even send Hubert Humphrey to Hickory Hill, if Ah thought it would do any good."

DOWN THE RAPIDS WITH BOBBY

I went down the rapids of the Colorado River in the Grand Canyon with Senator Robert Kennedy and his family and friends recently. There were 42 people in the party, including singer Andy Williams, mountain climber Jim Whittaker, pro-football player George Plimpton, skier Willy Schaeffler, publisher Otis Chandler, and 350 Kennedy children.

I was the only one in condition to make the trip, but in spite of this, my father didn't want me to go.

I assured him that the Kennedys would never do anything dangerous, but it was hard to persuade him. He said, "It's as safe to go down the Colorado River with Bobby Kennedy in a raft as it is to sail up the Nile with General Moshe Dayan."

Despite my father's fears, I'm glad I went. You really don't get to know a man until you've taken a rapid with him. The trouble is, Bobby Kennedy took a lot of rapids, and he took them on an air mattress. Ethel, mother of ten, also took the rapids out of the raft, and of course, her children took the rapids out of the raft, so there was nothing left for the rest of the party to do but leave the raft as well.

The best way to take a rapid is to float feetfirst on your life preserver, just in case you hit a rock. But I invented a new way of doing it. If you keep your mouth open, you can swallow most of the water you're going over, which makes it half as rough. My wife had to give me mouth-to-mouth resuscitation every night when we camped, but no one noticed it because everyone thought we were just kissing under the stars.

If you're ever going down the rapids with the Kennedys, it's best to choose a river that isn't surrounded by cliffs. Every morning after breakfast Bobby would look up at a mountain and ask Mount Everest climber Jim Whittaker, "Do you think it's tough to climb?" If Whittaker said no, Bobby would look at another mountain. "What about that one?"

If Whittaker said, "It's impossible," Bobby would call the party together and say, "That's the one we're going up," and pretty soon Ethel, mother of ten, the Kennedy children, and the rest of the group would be scrambling up the mountain in 110-degree heat.

After the mountain had been conquered, everyone would return to the rafts to take some more rapids. By the third day I was starting to have a great deal of respect for my father, and I wouldn't take off my life preserver, even to get into my sleeping bag.

Probably the most dangerous part of the trip was the last day, when we arrived at a place laughingly called Phantom Lodge, seven miles down, at the bottom of the Grand Canyon. The only ways to get out of the canyon are to walk out in 119-degree heat, ride a burro out along the same trail, or pretend you're going to die so they'll send a helicopter for you. I had rehearsed the death scene for three days, and by the time we arrived at Phantom Lodge, I was barely breathing.

Bobby opted to climb up the seven miles, as did the Kennedy children, and when Ethel, mother of ten, said she would climb out, too, the rest of the party was too embarrassed to say they'd rather go by helicopter.

Fearful that they would cancel the helicopter, I stopped breathing when Bobby and Jim Whittaker came up to me to see if they could persuade me to change my mind.

Bobby said, "Why don't you want to climb the mountain?"

I just smiled weakly and replied, "Because it's there."

※ ※ ※ ※ ※ ※ ※ ※ ※ ※ ※ ※ ※ ※ ※

4

LIVE AND IN COLOR

ADDING INSULT TO INJURY

Every time you think television has hit its lowest ebb, a new type program comes along to make you wonder where you thought the ebb was. The latest in TV wrinkles is what could be termed the insult interview show, in which the interviewer spends two or three hours insulting his guests. Joe Pyne is probably the master of this type of program, though, unfortunately, he now has many imitators. If you're lucky to live in a place that doesn't carry a show of this kind, they all go something like this:

INTERVIEWER: "Our next guest on *Couth Wants to Know* is Professor Kowowski. What do you do, Professor?"

PROFESSOR: "I am making a study of the world population explosion."

INTERVIEWER: "Well, that's the stupidest thing I've ever heard of. How did you ever get to be a professor?"

PROFESSOR: "I studied at Harvard, MIT, and did research at Stanford."

INTERVIEWER: "We've had lots of nuts on this show, but you take the cake. Tell us about the world population explosion."

PROFESSOR: "It is getting very serious. There will probably be a terrible crisis by 1990 which should wreak havoc on all mankind."

INTERVIEWER: "You sound like a pinko to me. Who gives you money for your research—the Soviet Union?"

PROFESSOR: "May I continue?"

INTERVIEWER: "Sure. We may not get a kook like you again."

PROFESSOR: "The main problem is that the population is increasing at a much faster rate than our food production."

INTERVIEWER: "Well, what about all those nutty kids at Berkeley?"

PROFESSOR: "I beg your pardon?"

INTERVIEWER: "You're a professor. Why can't you keep those nutty kids on the campuses in line?"

PROFESSOR: "I'm not interested in that problem."

INTERVIEWER: "Of course you're not. You're so wrapped

up in your miserable statistics you don't even know what's going on in the world. You know what I would do if I was a professor and the kids got out of line?"

PROFESSOR: "What?"

INTERVIEWER: "I'd shoot them. I carry a gun with me at all times, and if I found a kid who gave me a bad time, I'd just take out the gun and put one right between his eyes. You want to see my gun?"

PROFESSOR: "Not particularly."

INTERVIEWER: "Well, here it is. It's a .38 revolver, and I don't mind telling you they'd better not mess with me."

PROFESSOR: "I thought we were going to discuss the population explosion."

INTERVIEWER: "You eggheads give me a pain. I don't care about the population explosion, and I don't think anybody watching this show cares. I'm sorry we even asked you on the show."

PROFESSOR: "Well, I'll be happy to leave."

INTERVIEWER (*picking up the gun*): "Not before the commercial break. What do you feel is the solution to the population explosion?"

PROFESSOR: "Strong birth-control measures."

INTERVIEWER: "Don't you have any shame?"

PROFESSOR: "What do you mean by that?"

INTERVIEWER: "You mentioned the words 'birth control' on a family show. I've got a good mind to pop you in the nose, but we have to pause for a commercial. Stay tuned, folks, to this informative, thought-provoking show that is not afraid to deal with controversial subjects and let the chips fall where they may."

NO, VIRGINIA, THERE ISN'T

When the late President Kennedy canceled his subscription to the New York *Herald Tribune,* I wrote a letter to my little friend, Virginia, assuring her that although the paper wasn't read in the White House, it was still very much alive and would remain alive as long as there were Presidents in the White House to cancel their subscriptions to it.

I recently received another letter from Virginia. It read:

DEAR SIR:

I am seven years old, and all my friends tell me there is no New York *Herald Tribune*. I won't believe it's so, until I read it in your column. Are they lying again?

Your friend,
VIRGINIA

DEAR VIRGINIA:

Unfortunately, this time your friends are telling the truth. The reason there is no *Trib* is that it could exist no longer. No, Virginia, there is no *Herald Tribune*. You are too young to understand why it is no more, and so am I.

The publishers said they wanted to publish it, but the unions wouldn't let them. The unions said they wanted to print it, but the publishers wouldn't let them. The advertisers all insisted New York City needed a *Herald Tribune,* but many of them wouldn't advertise in it. The readers said the New York *Herald Tribune* was a great newspaper, but apparently there just weren't enough of them.

Everyone loved the *Herald Tribune,* even the competitors, but that did not prevent it from dying. Alas, Virginia, how dreary New York will be without the *Trib,* as dreary as many other cities where newspapers have died, and none have come to take their place.

A newspaper is not like Santa Claus. You don't have to see Santa Claus to know he exists, but you have to see a newspaper. You have to touch it and feel it and read it and, what's even more, believe in it.

A newspaper cannot be published on faith alone. It needs editors, reporters, printers, technicians, advertisers, distributors, and readers, and if you can't have all these, you can't have a paper, at least not for very long.

No *Herald Tribune*. It's true, Virginia. Those of us who worked for it thought it would live for a thousand, nay, ten thousand years from now. We thought it would gladden the hearts of Virginias for generations to come. We didn't believe it would disappear until it happened, and some of us can't believe it still.

I'm sorry to break the news to you in this way, but although your friends were right, tell them not to gloat when a newspaper dies. A little of the truth, beauty, romance, love, faith, and fancy that the world is so short of dies with it.

Sincerely,
A.B.

THERE'S GOOD NEWS TONIGHT

Both President Johnson and Vice-President Hubert Humphrey have been bitterly complaining lately over the lack of good news being reported by American newspapermen. They both have contended that the American image is being hurt abroad because all that people have been reading lately is the bad news about the United States.

They certainly have a point, and every responsible newspaper is now hiring a "good news" editor, who is responsible for getting as much good news in the paper as possible. So far, they've had a hard time ferreting out many good news stories, but it isn't for lack of trying. Here are some of the kinds of stories they're looking for.

HOUSTON, Tex.—Private Muhammad Ali, otherwise known as Cassius Clay, was awarded the good conduct medal today after being in the U.S. Army for only two weeks. Private Muhammad said, "All I want to be is a good soldier and make Pfc." Asked if he missed fighting for the world heavyweight championship, Private Muhammad said, "I'd rather fight the Vietcong any day."

MONTGOMERY, Ala.—Governor Lurleen Wallace cut the three hundredth ribbon today to open another integrated school in Alabama. The governor said, "I won't rest until every school in Alabama is completely free of discrimination, but I don't think I could have done it without the support of my husband, George, and the good people of the state of Alabama."

DETROIT, Mich.—Ralph Nader announced today that every new model car coming off the assembly line this year was completely safe and accident-proof. He told the American Society of Automobile Manufacturers that he was proud of the way they had accepted all his safety suggestions. He particularly cited the good faith of General Motors for its cooperation during the past year. The manufacturers presented Nader with their Man of the Year Award in gratitude for his pointing out their shortcomings to the American consumer.

WASHINGTON, D.C.—The National Rifle Association called for strong legislation this week to prevent guns from getting into the hands of an unsuspecting public. A spokesman for the organization said, "Guns in themselves are dangerous and should be handled only by the few discerning people who are experienced with them. The hackneyed argument for the ownership of guns goes back to the Constitution; but it is a faulty one, and if we can't stop people from buying guns, then the Constitution should be changed."

CAMBRIDGE, Mass.—Secretary of State Dean Rusk told the Harvard graduating class this morning that the United States had made many mistakes in the handling of the Vietnam war and that he could see why Hanoi didn't want to go to the conference table at this time. He said he thought the antiwar demonstrators, as well as the speeches by Senator Fulbright and Senator Kennedy, were very helpful in bringing about a peaceful settlement to the conflict, and he only wished more people would speak out against the war. The Harvard students threw flowers in front of the Secretary's limousine as he left the campus.

LANGLEY, Va.—The CIA announced today that it was giving up its role as an espionage organization and would devote its efforts in the future to medical research. In explaining the agency's decision, Richard Helms told newspapermen, "Spying is a dirty business, and the CIA wants no part of it."

WASHINGTON, D.C.—President Johnson called a press conference today and attacked the press for printing only the good news coming out of Washington. He pointed out that because there was no bad news being reported, the public was interpreting his good news as bad news.

Merriman Smith said, "Thank you, Mr. President."

BACKGROUNDERS ARE GOOD FOR YOU

There has been criticism of the press recently for attending what is known in Washington parlance as the backgrounder. The backgrounder is an anonymous press conference at which some high official reveals certain "facts" to the press on the condition that the reporters will not identify the source of their news.

The trouble with this type of briefing is that it not only

puts the newspaperman under obligation to the official for holding the backgrounder, but also is used as a method of sending up trial balloons which many times are filled with hot air.

I hadn't realized the role backgrounders played in the life of the average newspaperman in Washington until I had my foot up on the bar at the National Press Club one night and overheard the following conversation between four top flight Washington correspondents.

The first one said, "A reliable source reported to me this morning that the State Department will soon merge with the U.S. Coast Guard as an economy measure, as well as a practical matter."

"I checked this out with a high-level spokesman at the White House," the second reporter said, "and he denied it."

"How high was your high-level spokesman?" the first reporter demanded.

"He was a damned sight higher than your reliable source at the State Department," the second man replied.

"It doesn't make any difference who outranks whom," the third man said, "because I just spoke to an informed source at the Pentagon, not for attribution, of course, and he told me off the record that he could not comment on it, which certainly makes one believe there is something to it."

The fourth man became highly agitated. "A government spokesman who backgrounded us this morning said it was his understanding that State was going to merge with Health, Education, and Welfare and the U.S. Coast Guard was going to become part of the Library of Congress."

The first man spoke up again. "It so happens that a well-informed unnamed Administration official told us that your government official's backgrounder was in complete contradiction to an 'unidentified story' he released to the press earlier in the day."

"Oh, yeah, wise guy?" the fourth man said. "Your well-informed Administration official is noted for leaking denials of other people's backgrounders, and I wouldn't put any faith in anything he said."

"You'd talk differently if you knew who my well-informed Administration official is. He chews up government officials for breakfast."

The third man chimed in, "I always get my stories on highest authority."

"Sure, but you attribute any reliable source to the highest authority."

"I have more faith in them than I do in top U.S. officials."

"The other day you even quoted an informed official as an authoritative source."

"That's still better than what you did when you got a story from someone 'in touch with the Pentagon' and changed it to 'a source close to the White House.'"

"I had permission to change it."

"From whom?"

"A highly placed official. Who else?"

LIVE AND IN COLOR

When it was first revealed at a radio and TV newscasters' conference that, thanks to communications satellites, we would soon be able to see live television coverage of the Vietnam war, it was probably one of the great breakthroughs in TV. No longer would we have to wait one or two days to see filmed reports of what had taken place out there. Soon we could sit back in our armchairs and relax and watch a play-by-play of the war as it was happening!

"Good evening, ladies and gentlemen. The Consolidated Broadcasting Company is proud to present live and in color another great day in the Vietnam war. Our reporters are standing by in strategic spots all over the country to bring you the on-the-spot fighting as it takes place. But before we go to the battlefield, let's talk about real beer flavor. . . .

"Well, we're back in Vietnam, and Starkley Van Heusen is wading through the rice paddies of the Mekong Delta. Take it away, Starkley."

"Thanks, Jack. I'm with the Two Hundred and Thirty-fourth Lowland Brigade, and in a few minutes we're going to attack that village over there. It's believed to contain a company of Vietcong, and our boys are anxious to clean them out. We should be treated to some pretty good fighting in the next few minutes. There they go. As you can see, they're moving up now with their flame throwers and machine guns. Let's ask this sergeant here how he sees the results. Sarge, would you like to make a comment on the attack?"

"Blankety, blank, blank, blank, and blank."

"Sorry about that, folks, but that's one of the hazards of broadcasting the war, any war, live on television."

"Excuse us, Starkley, we're going to have to break away at this time for a commercial. You know, folks, if you ever get a queasy feeling when you wake up in the morning and. . . .

"Now back to live action here in Vietnam. We've just received word that an air strike is in progress over Kumithi, and Art Calgon is along for the story."

"Thanks, Jack. I'm sitting in the back of a dive bomber, and as you people can see, it's just beautiful up here. We should be in for quite a thrill, as this is the first time in history that American television audiences will witness an actual bombing of a Vietnamese village, live and in color. So sit back and relax, folks, as we pour it on Kumithi.

"First we'll just buzz the village to show you how it looks before the bombing, and then we'll give you a chance to see it after the bombing. Here we go into our dive—one, two, three, four bombs away! Look at those huts go up in flames. Now let's see that on the stop-action instant-replay camera again. That's what you call being in the catbird seat. Have we got time for a strafing run, Jack?"

"Sorry, Art, we don't have time for strafing today. Maybe we'll try it tomorrow. In the meantime let's talk about household insurance. Are you getting the best buy. . . .

"Well, we've just shown you two highlights of today's war. That should have done it, but we're in luck. Our Danang man, Jim Killian, reports the Vietcong have just launched a mortar attack on the airport, so let's see what that looks like."

"Thank you, Jack. This is Jim Killian, and as you can see, folks, we're under heavy attack from the Vietcong."

"Jim, could you get your camera a little higher? The viewers back home can't see too well what is going on."

"I've got it as high as I can, Jack. They're lobbing them in pretty heavy."

"What kinds of mortars are they, Jim? I'm sure the people would like to know."

"It beats me."

"Well, while you're finding out, Jim, we'll hear a few words about a laundry detergent that really gets clothes white. . . ."

KARATE AND THE JAPANESE DRIVER

There seems to be general agreement among all world travelers that there is nothing on earth to compare with the Tokyo traffic or the Japanese driver.

The traditional samurai-kamikaze spirit which has been passed on from father to son now manifests itself on the streets of the world's largest city. The most noble act that a licensed Japanese driver can perform is to crash his car into flames at an intersection, taking as many other cars with him as he possibly can.

The Japanese practice a form of vehicular karate which is not only a sport but a form of self-defense. It is known as "the way," and it is believed the true meaning of life can be found only after a person has experienced a traffic pileup in the rain on the Ginza at six o'clock in the evening.

A qualified karate driver must show courage, determination, and spirit. His mind must be cleared of all thoughts, and he must be prepared at all times, not only to defend his car, but also to attack another car when the opportunity presents itself.

He also must master "the absence of preconceived thoughts." Each traffic situation must be treated as a brand-new one, requiring a self-confidence that can come only from long hours of meditation during the endless Tokyo traffic jams.

In order to qualify for a black safety belt, the driver must learn to thrust, strike, block, heel, and twist his car, striking out at his opponent without worrying about the danger to his own safety or the consequences to those within a two-block radius of the traffic light.

A good karate driver must remain relaxed, the ball of his right foot firmly on the accelerator, the left foot near the brake. When he sees an opening, he makes a thrust toward it, screaming, *"Kiaii!"* This not only frightens the opponent in the other car, but also gives the driver the needed courage to go on.

At the moment the driver makes his thrust, his opponent may try to cut him off with a *uke-waza* (blocking technique). By braking fast, the driver uses the weight of his opponent's car against him, and with luck the other fellow will crash into a department-store window.

If the opponent manages to keep his car on the street, the karate driver must throw a *kake-uke* (inside hooking block), which can, with luck, make the opponent swerve into another oncoming car.

In order to keep their bumpers firm, most karate drivers practice on Tokyo pedestrians. A Japanese car in good condition can split three pedestrians in half with one blow. During my stay I was introduced to a ten-black-belt taxi driver who claimed he could split six pedestrians without hurting his cab.

The importance of karate driving to the Japanese cannot be underestimated. Not only does it build the spirit and soothe the mind, but it is also great for muscle toning, low blood pressure, and hardening the body.

It is Japan's greatest weapon against the population explosion, and many Japanese I spoke to say they prefer it to the pill.

5

✠ ✠ ✠ ✠ ✠ ✠ ✠ ✠ ✠ ✠ ✠ ✠ ✠ ✠

ONE-EYED MOSHE

HELP WANTED—EGYPTIAN OFFICERS

One of the fascinating offshoots of the Israeli-Arab war is the sudden interest now being shown by the different intelligence agencies in recruiting Egyptian military officers.

The Middle East is teeming with recruiters, all of whom are competing with one another for the services of the elite Egyptian Army and Air Force Corps.

My informant, who recently returned from Cairo, told me, "The CIA has a shopping list which calls for one hundred and fifty Egyptian generals and two hundred and thirty colonels. They'll even take more if they can get them."

"What does the CIA want to do with them?"

"It's my understanding that they want to drop them on North Vietnam to advise the Ho forces on how to win the war."

"What an ingenious scheme! With the Egyptians advising the North Vietnamese, the war will be over in no time."

"Exactly. But the CIA is having trouble. The Soviet Union also has a recruiting team in Cairo. They're trying to sign up the entire Egyptian general staff and send it through a third country into Red China. If they can get enough Egyptian generals working with the Red Chinese, the Russians can neutralize Red China without firing a shot."

"The Soviets are always trying to get into the act," I said.

"That isn't all. The Indians are trying to recruit some Egyptian officers to give to the Pakistanis as a gift, and the Albanians are trying to get an Egyptian general to head up the Yugoslav War College. There are so many demands being made for Egyptian military know-how, that Nasser is getting very worried."

"Why doesn't the CIA recruit its Egyptian officers from the ones captured by the Israelis in the war?"

"Because the Israelis are dead set against the Egyptian officers going back to any country other than Egypt."

"But why?" I asked.

"Nasser has promised that he will fight Israel again. The Israelis want the same Egyptian officers in command of Egypt's armed forces if hostilities break out again. This is why Israel is treating them so well. The Israelis are even making wholesale trades—ten thousand Egyptian officers for one Israeli corporal-cook—just so the Egyptian officers will be back at their commands before renewed fighting breaks out. As a matter of fact, the Israelis let many officers escape in the Sinai so they could return to Cairo and start rebuilding the army."

"Israel knows what it's doing," I said.

"The CIA is getting some of the stragglers, but the top officers, the ones who planned the defense of the Sinai, are hard to come by because they're so much in demand."

"Couldn't the CIA recruit Egyptian officers from those who can't return to Cairo because they handled their assignments so badly?"

"No. You see, in the retreat the generals who fouled up the most got to Cairo first, so they were able to tell their version of what happened before the rest of the Army got home. In order for Nasser to stay in power, he had to back them up. So the ones who goofed the most and have the greatest value to the intelligence agencies are still in their jobs."

"Wouldn't it be a wonderful world if all the armies were staffed by Egyptian officers?" I said.

"That," my informant said, "is the only solution to peace in our time."

THE ANGRY DOVE

The week since May 25 was a bad week for the doves and the hawks. Nasser's decision to close the Gulf of Aqaba to Israel had made hawks out of doves and doves out of hawks. The doves of the past wanted the United States to act immediately, and the hawks of Vietnam wanted us to cool it in the Middle East.

Even my friend Brinkerhoff, a devout pacifist, was in turmoil. When I saw him not long ago, he was sticking a knife into a photograph of Nasser and screaming, "Kill! Kill!"

"Brinkerhoff, how can you talk that way when you've been one of the leading advocates of peace in the world?"

"I'm still for peace in the world, but you'll never have it with that dirty rat, Nasser, in the Middle East. Kill!"

"Now, wait a minute, Brinkerhoff. If you're going to be a pacifist, you can't be going around screaming, 'Kill,' and stabbing photos of Nasser in the newspapers."

"That's how much you know about pacifists."

"Let me ask you this, Brinkerhoff. Would you advocate the use of force to reopen the Gulf of Aqaba to international shipping?"

"Only if we bomb Cairo first," Brinkerhoff said.

"But you're against bombing. Don't you remember, Brinkerhoff?"

"Stop telling me what I *was* against. Ask me what I'm for."

"All right, what are you for?"

"Blowing up the Aswan Dam, B-52 raids on the Suez Canal, and the complete defoliation of Jordan."

"If I didn't know you better, Brinkerhoff, I would think you've become a hawk."

"I'm not a hawk. I'm a dove who's lost his temper. I say there's only one solution to the Middle East crisis, and that's to escalate. Egypt must be made to pay for its aggression."

"But Brinkerhoff, the hawks in the United States say the matter should be settled peacefully in the United Nations."

"The hawks are chicken. The United Nations can't settle anything. The only thing the Arabs understand is force. We should nuke 'em."

"Nuke 'em?"

"Give 'em a taste of nuclear weapons, and let's see what big shots they are then."

"But, Brinkerhoff, you marched in a parade three weeks ago carrying a sign which said, 'Live and let live.' "

"I wasn't talking about Nasser and those Syrians. Besides, the United States has a commitment to Israel, and they should honor it."

"Do you think the United States should go it alone if nobody else wants to help?"

"You bet your sweet life they should go it alone. I say bomb them back to the Stone Age."

"Brinkerhoff, you sound like Barry Goldwater."

"What's wrong with Goldwater? At least he knows what a bunch of dirty double crossers the Russians are."

"Then you think we should stand up to the Russians on the question of the Middle East?"

"The hell with standing up to the Russians. Let's nuke 'em."

"I wish you wouldn't keep saying that, Brinkerhoff. It doesn't sound like you."

"You haven't heard anything yet," he said. "You know my son Herbert, the one who said he was going to be a draft dodger?"

"Yes. What about him?"

"Well, he's joining the U.S. Marine Corps. He says if we don't stop the Commies in the Middle East, we'll be fighting on the beaches of Coney Island."

"He said that?"

"Why do you look so surprised?" Brinkerhoff said. "Haven't you ever heard of the domino theory?"

HOW THE SOVIETS HELPED ISRAEL

There has been some confusion about how much aid the Soviet Union gave the Arab nations during the recent unpleasantness in the Middle East. What nobody knows is that the Soviets' real intention was to help Israel. But they had to do it in such a way that neither the Arab countries nor the West would find out about it.

It seems the Soviet Union has been trying to increase its arms business to compete with the United States and Great Britain. One of the most likely prospects was Israel, who was finding it hard to get military equipment from the West. The Soviets said they would give Israel everything she wanted, but it would have to be done in such a way that it wouldn't anger the Arab countries or even some Communist-leaning states.

Israel said she was interested but didn't want to do anything to anger the United States, Great Britain, and France.

Encouraged by what could turn out to be a very good customer, the Soviet Union proceeded to devise a way of getting Russian arms into the hands of the well-equipped Israeli Army. The big question was: How?

Then someone in the Politboro (the Soviets refuse to say who) got a brilliant idea. He told the Israeli diplomats, "We naturally cannot sell you the weapons directly; but why don't we give them to the United Arab Republic, and then you can get our weapons from them?"

The Israelis pointed out that the UAR might be reluctant to give the Israelis any of their Soviet weapons. The Soviets told them not to worry about it. "Just give us a list of what you need," they said.

The Israelis, trusting implicitly in the good faith of the Soviet Union, handed in a list, including tanks, guns, armored cars, jeeps, small arms, and, surprisingly enough, six or seven Soviet ground-to-air missiles.

A year later the Soviets told the Israelis that their order was ready and would be delivered in a month.

The Israelis were puzzled but decided to wait and see what would happen. Sure enough, in May, Gamal Abdel Nasser closed the Gulf of Aqaba and moved seven divisions of his troops and armor into the Sinai desert.

At the same time the Soviet Union accused Israel of being an "aggressor," which was the code name for "customer."

On June 5 the Israelis went to collect their equipment in the Sinai desert, where it was conveniently left by Egyptian troops, many of whom didn't even wait to be tipped for delivering it. The tanks, personnel carriers, guns, and even missiles were brand-new. A few were damaged in transit, but by and large the Russians had made everything available as ordered.

Some Soviet items accidentally left off the list were delivered to the Israelis, via Syria, a few days later.

All in all, it was quite a coup for the Soviet Union. In one of the great business deals of our time the Soviets managed to collect twice for the same equipment, first from the Arabs and then from the Israelis.

As a follow-up, it has been reported that the Soviets are sending in new arms and equipment to the United Arab Republic. What nobody knows is that all they're doing is filling another Israeli order for equipment. One Soviet diplomat told me, "By supplying the Arabs with arms, Israel has turned out to be the best customer we've got."

BUGGING HUSSEIN AND NASSER

It has been reliably reported that Israel listened in on telephone conversations between President Nasser and King Hussein while the war was going on. This, of course, was a violation of the Middle East antibugging laws, and we can expect the Soviet Union to bring it up in no uncertain terms at the United Nations.

While the Israelis published one such conversation that

they heard, there were others that took place during those four fateful days. I heard the tape of one the other day, and while I can't swear to its authenticity, it certainly sounded like Nasser and Hussein to me.

It went like this:

HUSSEIN: "Gamal, my brother and true defender, what the hell have you done to me? You made me lose Jerusalem, Bethlehem, and all the land west of the Jordan."

NASSER: "Well, nobody's perfect."

HUSSEIN: "I am not criticizing you, O hero of the Arab world and valiant conqueror of the Gulf of Aqaba, but that little piece of paper I signed with you last week also made me lose the Arab Legion."

NASSER: "Little king, do not despair. There is still much we can do."

HUSSEIN: "Such as what, O mighty prophet of the Sinai?"

NASSER: "Well, you can burn down the American Embassy for a start. I always find when I lose a war, that there's nothing like a good embassy fire to make people forget."

HUSSEIN: "A good idea, O God of the Gaza. I shall burn down the U.S. Embassy. Anything else?"

NASSER: "Then you must resign."

HUSSEIN: "But, Savior of the Suez, how can I resign?"

NASSER: "It is the only thing to do, my tiny sovereign. If you don't resign, the people will scream for your resignation. But if you do, they will shout for you to stay."

HUSSEIN: "How do you know this, O wise one?"

NASSER: "This isn't the first time I've lost a war."

HUSSEIN: "How true. You are known on everyone's lips as the loser of all time."

NASSER: "Now you flatter me."

HUSSEIN: "True leader of the Arab bloc, tell me, how do I explain the loss of Jerusalem to my people?"

NASSER: "Tell them American marines and British commandos wrested the city from your brave soldiers while the Israeli dogs cringed in their foxholes until the cease-fire was sounded."

HUSSEIN: "Of course. Why didn't I think of that?"

NASSER: "Obviously you've never lost Jerusalem before. You see, my fragile monarch, it isn't how you fight a war that counts, but what you say afterward that is important. Look at me. The Israelis took Gaza, the Sinai, Aqaba, and they are sitting on the Suez Canal. Yet the latest poll shows my popularity is at an all-time high."

HUSSEIN: "If you had only lost Cairo, you would live forever."

NASSER: "Say, by the way, Arab brother, I'm drawing up a new defense pact with Jordan. How about coming over this week to sign it?"

HUSSEIN: "O glorious deliverer, to think you still want to protect me after what you've done already."

NASSER: "Hush now. What good is a great UAR Army if it cannot offer assistance to a little friend?"

HUSSEIN: "How can I ever repay you?"

NASSER: "Could you lend me the use of an airplane until Thursday?"

DINNER CRISIS IN WASHINGTON

The breaking off of diplomatic relations between the Arab countries and the United States may have catastrophic results in Washington. Because the Arab embassies in this town did most of the entertaining, it is now predicted that 70 percent of all the important people in Washington may starve to death.

An evening never failed to go by that one Arab embassy or another didn't have a sumptuous dinner or cocktail party, and since the same people were always in attendance, many of them have been cut off from their only decent meal of the day.

Our society reporter in Washington, who never missed an Arab party, was found wandering in the streets, dazed and starving because she didn't have anyplace to go. The Red Cross has promised to take care of her until diplomatic relations with the Arab countries are resumed.

In the meantime, an emergency committee has been formed to take care of the thousands of other dinner guests who were innocent victims of the tragic events in the Middle East.

The Department of Agriculture has offered to supply food stamps to anyone who can produce a canceled invitation from an Arab embassy. The War on Poverty office has given out contracts to Washington caterers to provide hors d'oeuvres for famished Washington citizens, and every effort is being made to relocate couples at other embassy dinner parties where relations with the United States are still good.

One idea which is still under consideration is that if the Arab countries do not reestablish relations with the United States, the Arab embassies could be turned into carry-out shops, and people would be handed their food through a window.

Many people are blaming the Israeli Embassy for the dinner crisis in Washington. "The Israelis knew when they attacked Sinai that the Arab embassies wouldn't be able to serve dinners very long. They were obviously helped by British and American waiters."

One of the surprising results was that before the Middle East crisis turned into a war, the Soviet Embassy in Washington, which had provided all the caviar for Arab parties, had promised the Arabs that they would take over their entertaining in case the Middle East countries got into trouble. But now the Russians have backed away from their pledge and won't even give the Arabs a cup of sugar.

The United States, of course, is remaining mum during the dinner-shortage crisis. A spokesman for the State Department said, "All we want is peace on Embassy Row. We will remain neutral in word, deed, and thought." Later the White House said that it wasn't exactly neutral and that, although it would not get involved directly, it was still pledged to help anyone who ran out of plates.

Pressure is being brought to bear on the Israeli Embassy to fill the vacuum left by the departure of the Arab ambassadors and their wives. But an Israeli spokesman said, "We are a small embassy, and even if we wanted to take over the task of feeding all the people in Washington who were formerly fed by the Arabs, we wouldn't have enough tableclothes."

This throws the problem into the United Nations.

One diplomatic observer said, "The United Nations cannot stand idly by and see so many people left hungry and thirsty and without good dance music. If we can't save the social scene in Washington, who can?"

A GUIDE TO THE CRISIS

During the Middle East crisis I thought we ought to get our terms straight. It's very hard to understand what is going on unless you know what all the countries are talking about. So, as a public service, I am providing an instant definition guide to diplomatic language.

RESTRAINT—Something you tell another country to show when your own personal interests are not involved. It is usually urged by countries who would go to war in a minute if one of their enemies threatened war on them.

AGGRESSION—What the other side is committing at the time your side is trying to be a "peace-loving" nation—*i.e.*, the Russians claim the Israelis are committing aggression against the Arab world because Egypt has closed the Gulf of Aqaba to Israeli shipping.

A RECESS—Something that the Soviet delegate won't let Ambassador Arthur Goldberg have so Goldberg can go to the bathroom.

COMMITMENT—A commitment is a promise one nation gives another nation which it does or does not have to honor, depending on how the political wind is blowing. For example, the United States is fighting a war in Vietnam to honor its commitment in Southeast Asia. Because of this commitment, the Russians and Arabs are counting on the United States not to honor the one it has to Israel, since they believe the American people are sick and tired of honoring their country's commitments.

U.S. MILITARY AID—Something the United States gave to Jordan, Saudi Arabia, and Israel to maintain a balance of power there. If war comes to this area, American-made planes will be fighting American-made planes, U.S. antitank guns will try to knock out U.S. manufactured tanks, and American artillery shells will pass each other in the night.

COOLING-OFF PERIOD—A period advocated by U Thant to try to work out a solution to the mess he made when he pulled the UN troops out of Sinai and the Gulf of Aqaba without consulting the Security Council or the General Assembly.

A FACE-SAVING AND JUST SOLUTION FOR ALL PARTIES—That which every diplomat talks about, but nobody has any idea what the hell it is.

A UN RESOLUTION—if proposed by the United States, it will be automatically vetoed by the Soviet Union. If proposed by another country and passed, it will be ignored by the parties involved in the dispute. The violation of a UN resolution is used to justify an act of aggression.

ARAB UNITY—The pledge of all Arab countries to a united cause which could or could not last about two weeks. At this writing, Nasser has signed a military pact with King Hussein while Syria is calling for the chopping of Hussein's head.

DIPLOMATIC ACTIVITY—Actions taken by countries who don't know what action to take.

A SHOWDOWN—Something that observers believe neither Nasser nor the Soviet Union expected they would have at this time. The Israelis wanted to have it two weeks ago, but were persuaded to hold off by the United States because it was caught completely by surprise.

THE BRINK—That part of the precipice we keep returning to every time the Soviets think it's an opportune time to make another move.

WORLD WAR III—That which, because of the above definitions, we're on the brink of.

MEANWHILE, BACK AT THE RANCH . . .

Because of all the UN activity on television, a lot of us have been deprived of our favorite Westerns. The only thing for us to do is make up our own Western out of what has been happening in the Middle East and at the United Nations.

Fellow by the name of Jake owns a small piece of land where he's trying to farm and raise cattle. Trouble is, Jake's ranch is surrounded by a bunch of unfriendly landowners who keep sneaking on the property and sabotaging the wells and poisoning the horses.

These landowners are egged on by a large rancher named Red Boris who figures the more trouble he can cause among the small ranchers, the more embarrassing it will be for his arch rival, Big Sam, who owns a large piece of land down the way.

One day, at Red Boris' urging, a neighbor of Jake's named Abdullah cuts off Jake's water. When Jake raises cain about this, Abdullah just laughs and tells Jake if he tries to turn on the water, it will mean war.

Jake goes to see Big Sam, who's supposed to guarantee Jake's water rights. Jake tells Sam he's going to have to fight Abdullah if he doesn't get his water back.

Sam says that's no way to solve the problem. The way to solve it is to call a meeting of the Cattlemen's Association and work it out there.

Sam calls a meeting, and all the cattlemen show up. But no one seems too upset about Jake's water rights. Red Boris says Jake's just using the water shortage to attack all the ranchers in the area. Abdullah says Jake has no right to own a ranch in the area, and the other ranchers say Jake's been a trouble-maker since he moved in.

Big Sam says he's sympathetic to Jake's problem and tries to get other members of the Cattlemen's Association to support Jake.

But none of them shows much interest, and they all point out there's no sense going to war over Jake's water rights.

Jake listens to the discussions and figures by the time he gets any water, all his cattle will be dead. So one night he attacks Abdullah's ranch with a handful of cowboys. Abdullah's henchmen run for the hills, and Jake's men take back their water rights. In the meantime, Jake's other neighbors attack, and Jake, in true Western fashion, clobbers them. Pretty soon Jake finds himself holding land all around him that once belonged to his neighbors.

Red Boris, who wasn't much help to Abdullah, demands an emergency meeting of the Cattlemen's Association and demands that Jake be branded a horse thief, a cattle rustler, and a dirty varmit. Abdullah, who lost all the horses and guns Boris gave him, charges that Big Sam was the one who really attacked him, and Abdullah's pals all demand that Jake pull out from their land immediately.

Jake says he's tired of being pushed around, and before he pulls out, he wants some guarantees that Abdullah and his pals won't attack him again. He points out that when his water was cut off, the Cattlemen's Association didn't lift a finger to help him.

Big Sam is caught in the middle. He says Jake has to give up the land he took, but Abdullah has to recognize Jake's rights to his land, as well as his water. This, Abdullah says, he'll never do.

So Jake says the hell with it then. He'll just sit there.

What everyone is worried about is that Red Boris and Big Sam may get into a real gunfight over the situation and wipe the whole valley out.

So everyone says the Cattlemen's Association has to settle

the matter to everyone's satisfaction. But if you've seen any cowboy pictures before, you know this is damn well impossible.

ONE-EYED MOSHE

There is no doubt that a movie will be made on the recent Israeli-Arab war. Two producers have already submitted titles. Darryl Zanuck wants to call his *The Shortest Day,* and Otto Preminger would title his *Son of Exodus.*

A third company is also thinking about a film called *One-Eyed Moshe,* but the reason they can't go into production is that they're having script trouble.

When the screenwriter submitted his story outline to the producer, the producer called him in and angrily said, "What kind of a nut do you think I am? The public will never believe the Israelis took Egypt, Jordan, and Syria in four days."

"I knew it sounded silly when I wrote it, chief, but it's based on fact. We can't fool with history."

"Who says we can't? John Wayne, Kirk Douglas, and Gregory Peck couldn't take Egypt, Jordan, and Syria in four days. Where's the conflict?"

"Well, I've tried to weave a fictitious story in there. You see, we have a one-eyed general, played by Sammy Davis, Jr., of course, and his driver, an Israeli sergeant, played by Frank Sinatra. The picture starts off in Tel Aviv with the general telling his driver to take him to the front. In the next shot we see them in Gaza. This is before the titles."

"They've taken Gaza, and we haven't even had the titles yet? You must be out of your mind."

"In Gaza, Sinatra meets Elizabeth Taylor, who plays an Israeli machine gunner. She asks General Moshe if she can go with him to the front. The general says all right but asks her to keep her head down. The next scene they're in the Sinai desert, and they've captured an Egyptian armored division commanded by Omar Sharif.

"Sharif is wounded, and Sinatra wants to kill him. But Taylor insists on nursing him back to health. Sharif is put in the jeep with General Moshe, and they drive off for the front."

"The jeep's getting kind of crowded, isn't it?"

"Now hear me out, chief. They all arrive at the Suez Canal, and Taylor, who is hot and dirty, decides to take a swim in the canal. But she doesn't have a bathing suit. So she makes everyone turn his back, except for General Moshe, who only has to put his hand over his good eye. Taylor goes into the water.

"While they've got their eyes shut, Sharif steals a pistol out of the jeep and is about to shoot General Moshe and Sinatra when Dean Martin jumps Sharif and wrestles the pistol out of his hand."

"Where did Dean Martin come from?"

"He was a drunken Suez Canal boat pilot left over from 1956. He says he's been trying to get home ever since. So they take him along with them and drive down to the Gulf of Aqaba, where Paul Newman is in command. It turns out Taylor was an old girl friend of Newman's, but he married Eva Marie Saint, a Gentile woman who stayed in Israel after Otto Preminger made *Exodus.*

"Sinatra wants to kill him, too, but before he gets a chance, General Moshe orders everyone back into the jeep to take him to Old Jerusalem, where Peter O'Toole personally surrenders the Arab Legion to General Moshe. Sharif, realizing the war is lost, surrenders, too, and Sinatra offers him an Israeli cigarette, showing that even in war all men are brothers.

"Taylor, seeing Sinatra's gesture, puts down her machine gun and kisses him while both the Arabs and the Israelis cheer.

"Then General Moshe jumps back into his jeep and yells, 'Take me to Damascus!'

"The picture ends with the jeep heading up into the Syrian hills with Taylor riding on a fender and Sharif and O'Toole waving good-bye."

"Okay," the producer says. "If it doesn't work, we can always sell it to television."

�✗✗✗✗✗✗✗✗✗✗✗✗✗✗

I WANT A PAPER DOLL

THE CHIC TOURIST

The new summer fashions for American tourists visiting Washington have recently been released, and from all indications the clothes are going to be more formal than in previous years.

The source of this information was Sophie Glutz, the famous Washington tourist fashion expert, who said, "It appears now that women will be wearing more stretch pants than Bermuda shorts when visiting the public monuments."

"How do you explain it?" I asked.

"I guess they've all been influenced by Mrs. Johnson's beautification program."

"Does this mean that women tourists visiting this town will no longer be wearing blue jeans and sweat shirts?"

"Oh, I wouldn't rule that out completely. In the daytime you may find a certain amount of women in blue jeans and sweat shirts, as well as shorts, but in the evening they will probably change into slacks, stretch pants, and blouses."

"Is it true that the short shorts are out?"

"They are after four o'clock. Of course, many tourists will still visit the White House and the Lincoln Memorial in short shorts, but we're recommending longer shorts for the Senate and House of Representatives."

"I think that's wise," I said. "What about skirts?"

"Skirts are awfully dressy for sightseeing in Washington, but some women will wear them with halters and bare midriffs and open-toed sandals."

"What about dresses and suits for women?"

"Heaven forbid. A woman tourist wouldn't be seen dead in a dress or suit. All the other tourists would laugh at her."

"What about styles?"

"Keeping your hair in curlers while sightseeing still seems to be the rage. The large colored plastic curlers which stick out all over your head are coming back in again."

"How about face cream?"

"It's optional. Many women tourists prefer it to suntan oil as suntan oil doesn't show up as well."

"I suppose socks and stockings are out?"

"They have been for some time now, unless you're going to a state dinner at the White House."

"What's new in colors?"

"In shorts, we're recommending plaids for women who weigh more than one hundred and fifty pounds. They look so much better from the rear. Also, stripes are back in, at least as far as sweat shirts are concerned. The simple black toreador pants of a few years ago are definitely out."

"What about men's tourist fashions?"

"There hasn't been too much change in men's fashions this year. They'll still wear Army fatigues, bright-colored sports shirts, sneakers, and baseball caps."

"And children?"

"We're not laying down any hard and fast rules on what children should wear in Washington. The National Gallery of Art has asked that children not wear bathing suits when visiting it, but you have to remember that the gallery is a very stuffy institution."

"I'm delighted to see how the standards in clothes have gone up in the nation's capital this year," I said.

"Yes, it's amazing how clothes-conscious Americans are when they visit Washington these days. It's as though they know that they're on display, and they want to look their best for the Great Society."

I WANT A PAPER DOLL

Has it ever occurred to you that the newspaper you read could easily be made into a dress? The thought hadn't occurred to me until one evening when my wife was getting dressed for a party and the children were jumping up and down in the bedroom.

"Be careful, children," she said, "or you'll tear my dress off."

"What kind of talk is that?" I wanted to know.

"Well, it's true," my wife said. "This is a paper dress, and I don't want it ripped before I get to the party."

"What's the advantage of wearing a paper dress?"

"You only have to wear it once, and then you can throw it away."

"But you do that with all your clothes anyway," I said. "There's nothing new about that."

She ignored my remark. "What do you think?"

"I like every part of it except by your hips, where it says, 'All the news that's fit to print.' "

"It's woven into the pattern," she replied. "There's nothing I can do about it."

"You could at least have bought a dress with my column in it," I complained bitterly.

"I think that would be very pretentious. Besides, I think James Reston goes so much better with my shoes."

We arrived at the party and found six or seven other women wearing paper dresses. One lady was causing a sensation.

"Where did you get it?" everyone wanted to know.

"District News was having a sale on *Playboy* magazines, so I bought several yards of them and had my dressmaker sew them together."

"How did you manage to get the fold out to fit so perfectly?" one of the men wanted to know.

One woman was wearing *Newsweek* magazine, another had on *Esquire,* and a third woman was wearing the *Atlantic Monthly.* But the woman who made the biggest hit was the one who was wearing a dress made from the *Reader's Digest.*

"It's lovely," someone exclaimed.

"I was very lucky," the woman said. "I'm a very small size."

People started dancing, and my wife seemed to be having a wonderful time, so I cut in on her.

"I heard what that fellow was singing," I said angrily.

"What?" she wanted to know.

"He was singing, 'I want a paper doll that I can call my own.' "

"Stop being so jealous," she said. "It's all in fun."

"He also put his hand on 'All the news that's fit to print.' "

"You're imagining things. His hand never left the photo of President Johnson in Bethesda Naval Hospital."

"Well, I think paper dresses are very provocative, and I wish you'd go back to your topless evening gown," I said.

"This is a nice gray dress, and it's nothing for you to be ashamed of."

"I'm getting tired of everyone saying I'm a paper tiger," I told her.

OF MICE AND WOMEN

Scientists are worried about the new fashions in women's clothes and their effects on the human male. The short skirts, the topless evening gowns, and the bare bathing suits will soon be very commonplace, and no one knows how much further the male can be pushed before he loses control.

One scientist who has been studying the problem is Professor Heinrich Applebaum of the Advanced Institute for Provocative Behavior.

I visited the learned professor in his laboratory, and he told me in a thick German accent, which I'll spare you, "We are reaching a threshold in clothes which could change the behavior patterns of every man and woman in the modern world."

"How's that, Professor?"

"Well, let me show you. Naturally, I cannot work with human beings, as it is still too dangerous. So I have been doing my experiments with mice. Over here in this cage you see a female mouse and three male mice. Now the female mouse has a normal skirt which just covers her four knees. The male mice are relaxed and quiet."

"They don't even seem to notice the female mouse," I said.

"That's correct. Now I'm going to change the skirt on the female mouse so that it will be several millimeters above her knees. I place her back in the cage."

"The male mice are becoming very agitated," I exclaimed.

"Exactly. They can't even work. Their pulse rate has gone up; their breathing is no longer normal."

"They're running around in circles," I said.

"Now let us raise the skirt even higher, almost to the thigh."

"The male mice's eyes are bugging out."

"Note that two of them are frothing at the mouth."

"You'd have to see it to believe it," I cried.

"Let us go over to this cage," Professor Applebaum said. "I'm going to put a topless bathing suit on this mouse. Note what happens to the male mice that are swimming in the tiny pool when the female mouse appears."

"Two of the male mice are drowning," I said.

"It happens every time. The males get so agitated they forget how to swim.

"These are female mice dressed in evening clothes. You will notice there are large holes cut in their dresses, and their bosoms are practically bare except for tiny Band-Aids. There is a little music box in the cage. When I turn on the music, the female mice will dance. Watch what happens to the male mice when I flip this switch."

"Heaven preserve us," I yelled. "The male mice have lost all control. They're chasing the female mice all over the cage."

"The males have passed what I call the sex threshold, which could be comparable to the sound barrier. There is no way of calming them down."

"Don't the female mice know what they have done?"

"They know, but they don't care."

"But if you translate this into human terms, it could mean —"

"Exactly," Professor Applebaum said. "We're nearing the sex threshold now. By summer we may have passed it."

"Look, there's one male mouse that isn't doing anything. Does that mean there's some hope?"

"No, he's blind. He was left over from our cigarette experiments."

PROSPERITY AND MINISKIRTS

My good friend Charlie Collingwood mentioned on the tube one night that during times of prosperity women's skirts get longer, but that during times of economic hardship skirts get shorter.

I wouldn't have given it a second thought, except that I happened to be in New York City the other day and I was walking down Fifth Avenue with my wife.

A girl in a miniskirt was walking toward us, and my eyes boggled. Naturally, my wife got angry. "You don't have to stare," she said.

"You wouldn't say that if you knew what I was doing," I said.

"I know very well what you're doing. You're filling your head with evil thoughts."

"That's not true," I said. "What I'm really doing is figuring out the stock market. If it's true that skirts go up during periods of recession, we may be in for a very bad time."

Another girl walked by with a skirt three inches above her knees. "Do you know what that tells me?" I asked my wife.

"I'd rather not guess," she retorted.

"It tells me I should sell my AT&T. But the question is, 'What should I buy instead?' "

"I'd suggest a pair of field glasses," she said.

"Now stop acting that way. If Charlie's theory is right, we stand to gain or lose a lot of money, and I should think you'd be as concerned as I am."

"Why don't you read the *Wall Street Journal* or subscribe to a financial newsletter like everybody else?"

"Because this method is foolproof. Look at that girl over there with her skirt almost up to her thighs. That could mean either of two things: tax-free bonds are going to be in demand, or the bottom is going to fall out of mutual funds."

"The bottom is going to fall out of something else if she tries to hail a cab," my wife said.

"You're letting your mind wander," I remonstrated. "These girls are trying to tell us something, if we only had the key."

Two ladies in miniskirts were looking into the Bergdorf Goodman window.

"Now what does that tell you?" my wife said angrily.

"Maybe I should sell short. They say the Dow-Jones averages can't go much higher."

"I wish the same could be said about the skirts."

"To most men," I explained, "miniskirts mean nothing more than a leg show. But when I see a miniskirt, I immediately think of Merrill Lynch Pierce Fenner & Smith."

"What about your other lecherous friends?"

"They're not lecherous friends. They're a brokerage house," I explained. "I'll bet they're out on the streets doing the same thing I'm doing right now."

We went by Saks Fifth Avenue, and my wife said she wanted to stop in for a moment. She suggested I study the industrials while I waited.

A half hour later she came out, wearing a miniskirt.

"What are you doing?" I cried.

"I've decided to play the market myself. If there's going to be a recession, I might as well be part of it while it lasts."

THE RED GUARDS ARE COMING

If anyone has any doubts that the country has gone daft, I would like to refer them to all the furor that has been raised in the newspapers and magazines over a seventeen-year-old Cockney model named Twiggy.

Twiggy, who appears to be the latest thing in sex symbols, looks like a boy. The only reason you know she's a girl is that her hair is cut much shorter than that of most seventeen-year-old boys.

Fashion designers may deny it, but I believe there is a conspiracy under way to destroy the female body as we know it. The object of the designers this year seems to be to make all women look like Al Capone, Ernest Hemingway, or Gunga Din.

This is not merely conjecture on my part. I recently visited the workroom of a fashion designer and interviewed him about what he was doing with women's fashions this year.

As I was ushered in, M. Alfonso came up to me.

"That's lovely, dear," he said, straightening the handkerchief in my pocket. "And the cigar is such a charming touch."

"M. Alfonso," his secretary cried, "this is not one of your models. He is a newspaperman."

"Forgive me," Alfonso begged. "I designed a lady's suit just like the one you're wearing, for teatime."

"Okay," I said, "anyone can make a mistake. Now, about the women's clothes that you people have been designing this year. Why are you making women look like men?"

"We're not making women look like men," Alfonso said. "We're liberating the female body from all the traditional garments that have made woman a second-class citizen for so many years."

Just then a model came in. She was wearing a fur hat, quilted jacket and pants, black boots, and two bandoliers loaded with ammunition over each shoulder. "I call this dress Partisan. It can be worn either to cocktails or for a small dinner party. I've designed a handbag that goes with it that is shaped like a machine gun."

"It sure looks sexy," I said.

He pushed a button, and another model walked in. She was dressed like an Army MP, including the silver helmet.

"This one is called Distinguished Service. You can wear it to lunch with or without the billy club. Jeanette, do I detect a bulge in front? Naughty, naughty, you know we're not showing bulges this year."

"Why aren't you showing bulges this year?" I demanded. "Men like women with bulges."

"But, my dear," he said, "bulges are so unsightly."

He pushed the button again, and what appeared to be a big game hunter walked in. She was wearing an Australian hat, a bush jacket, leather pants, heavy wool stockings, and chukka boots.

"I call this Dawn over Manitoba. You can wear it at home when you're having guests in."

"M. Alfonso, I don't mean to sound critical, but these clothes certainly don't do much for a woman's figure."

"Of course not. That's the Red Guard influence. I studied the pictures of the Chinese Red Guards day after day, and then it came to me. You couldn't tell the women from the men. I don't know how the Chinese ever thought of it."

At that moment what I took to be a model walked in wearing a black leather raincoat, tall brown boots, and a red helmet with a number on it.

"What's that?" I asked.

"I'm not sure," he said nervously. "We're either having a fire or previewing my latest wedding dress."

SAM, YOU MADE THE SKIRT TOO LONG

It appears from all the fashion reports and magazines that women are going to be wearing pants this year. Not just slacks or pedal pushers or pajamas, but real pants. The pants suit for women has come into its own, and the question about who wears the pants in the family is no longer very funny.

Where will it all end?

The first man to actually wear a skirt in public was Horace Gringsby, an advertising executive, who on October 20, 1967, showed up at his office in one—half as a joke and half as a protest gesture because all the women in his office were wearing pants.

After everyone had his laugh and made his snide remarks, curiosity got the better of a few of the men in the office, and one asked, "How does it feel?"

"Quite comfortable," Horace admitted. "Your legs have much more freedom, and it's a lot cooler than pants."

"But don't you have to shave your legs?" someone else asked.

"I suppose so. But it's easier than keeping a crease in your pants."

The following week several of the men started wearing skirts, and the agency was getting a name for itself.

But then some smart-aleck cop arrested Horace and charged him with impersonating a woman. Horace, who had played center on the Yale football team, took the case to the Supreme Court, which in a historic five to four ruling said there was nothing wrong with a man's wearing a skirt as long as he didn't yell, "Fire," in a crowded theater.

Pretty soon skirts for men were being featured in *Esquire*, *Playboy* magazine, and *Men's Wear Daily*.

The college male students bought skirt and sweater sets, the Brooks Brothers crowd went for navy blue and slate gray skirt suits, and on the West Coast the surfers started wearing miniskirts over their bathing suits.

But while the change was welcome, something still didn't look right. Then someone realized that men's shoes didn't look good with skirts, so a shoe company in Chicago introduced high heels to go with the new outfits. This made all the difference, and in no time at all men were wearing high heels to go with their skirts.

One of the complaints, though, was that in winter the men's legs got cold. So a men's hosiery manufacturer put out a line of nylon stockings with a garter belt attached to men's shorts. There was such a run on them at first that they had to be rationed—one pair to a customer.

While the lower half now looked very attractive, most men felt they could dress up the upper half of their outfits. A few started wearing necklaces, some put on bracelets, and still others started wearing earrings.

The jewelry didn't look too good against short hair, so many men started to let their hair grow below their shoulders, or if this wasn't possible, they wore wigs.

Men were spending fortunes on hairdressers and also cosmetics, first rouge and then lipstick and finally nail polish.

As the emphasis on men's clothes and appearance became

greater, more and more department stores turned over their space to them, and millions of dollars of advertising budgets were switched to the male market. The Paris designers and the Seventh Avenue manufacturers gave up making female clothes, as there was no money in it.

In the short span of ten years it became a man's world. And what happened to women during this period? They kept walking around in pants and nobody ever bothered to look at them again.

✖ ✖ ✖ ✖ ✖ ✖ ✖ ✖ ✖ ✖ ✖ ✖ ✖ ✖

7

E-E-E-E-KONOMICS

EVERYONE IS MERGING

Every time you pick up the newspaper you read about one company merging with another company. Of course, we have laws to protect competition in the United States, but one can't help thinking that if the trend continues, the whole country will soon be merged into one large company.

It is 1978, and by this time every company west of the Mississippi will have merged into one giant corporation known as Samson Securities. Every company east of the Mississippi will have merged under an umbrella corporation known as the Delilah Company.

It is inevitable that one day the chairman of the board of Samson and the president of Delilah would meet and discuss merging their two companies.

"If we could get together," the president of Delilah said, "we would be able to finance your projects and you would be able to finance ours."

"Exactly what I was thinking," the chairman of Samson said.

"That's a great idea, and it certainly would make every one's life less complicated."

The men shook on it, and then they sought approval from the Antitrust Division of the Justice Department.

At first the head of the Antitrust Division indicated that he might have reservations about allowing the only two companies left in the United States to merge.

"Our department," he said, "will take a close look at this proposed merger. It is our job to further competition in private business and industry, and if we allow Samson and Delilah to merge, we may be doing the consumer a disservice."

The chairman of Samson protested vigorously that merging with Delilah would not stifle competition but would help it. "The public will be the true beneficiary of this merger," he said. "The larger we are, the more services we can perform, and the lower prices we can charge."

The president of Delilah backed him up. "In the Communist system the people don't have a choice. They must buy from the state. In our capitalistic society the people can buy from either the Samson Company or the Delilah Company."

102

"But if you merge," someone pointed out, "there will be only one company left in the United States."

"Exactly," said the president of Delilah. "Thank God for the free enterprise system."

The Antitrust Division of the Justice Department studied the merger for months. Finally, the Attorney General made this ruling: "While we find some drawbacks to only one company's being left in the United States, we feel the advantages to the public far outweigh the disadvantages.

"Therefore, we're making an exception in this case and allowing Samson and Delilah to merge.

"I would like to announce that the Samson and Delilah Company is now negotiating at the White House with the President to buy the United States. The Justice Department will naturally study this merger to see if it violates any of our strong antitrust laws."

WALL STREET AND PEACE

STOCK PRICES DIVE ON NEW RUMORS OF PEACE FEELERS— Headline in the Washington *Post*.

As someone who watches the stock market every day with trepidation, I was very nervous when I read the news that false rumors about Hanoi peace feelers had sent the market into a decline. I'm as much for peace as anybody in this country, but if it's going to have a serious adverse effect on Wall Street, I think we'd better think twice about any kind of negotiations.

The minute I read the story, I called my broker and said, "What gives with the peace feelers from Hanoi?"

He said, "It could be just a scare. Our information is that peace is still far away, but people are running scared."

"Thank God, it's only a rumor," I said. "I'd hate anything to interfere with my investments."

"I don't blame you," he said. "I wouldn't have put you in all those defense stocks if I thought there was any chance of a settlement in South Vietnam."

"Listen, while I've got you on the phone, Russia has just asked for a treaty to internationalize the moon. It sounds like a peace gesture to me. Maybe I'd better sell."

"I'm not sure. The next day the Russians warned us to

keep our mitts off Cuba. It came at the right time, too, because the moon business could have caused a selling wave."

"Well, if you ask me, the Russians have been too damned conciliatory lately, and it isn't helping my portfolio at all."

"I think you're being pessimistic about this," my broker said. "It's true that there haven't been too many war scares recently as far as the Soviets are concerned, but we're still a long way from peace."

"Don't you think Castro's acting up the way he has will help my investments?"

"It might, except Castro is having so much trouble with Red China. The thinking down here on the street is that Castro won't affect the market one way or the other."

"Getting back to Vietnam," I said. "What do you make of these Buddhist demonstrations?"

"If you want my personal opinion, it should be good for the stock market. As long as the South Vietnamese can't get together, there doesn't seem to be much hope for a peaceful settlement in the country, and if that's so, the bulls are going to come out ahead."

"I figured as much. But this is what has me worried. If a rumored peace feeler from Hanoi can send the Dow-Jones average down twelve points, why couldn't the Communists announce a real peace offer and send Wall Street into a crash?"

"Don't you think we haven't thought of it," my broker said. "But I don't think the Communists would be that smart.

"Besides, as long as we have to contain Red China, the stock market should remain steady. You can't worry about these day-to-day fluctuations caused by a lot of silly peace talk."

"One more question," I said. "I hear relations between the U.S. and France are getting worse. That's a good thing, isn't it?"

"Very good. Do you want to buy anything on margin?"

YOU HAVE A FRIEND

The tight money market has caused a complete switch in the thinking of our nation's banks. There was a time when bankers were on their knees begging people to borrow money from them, and everyone had a "friend" at the bank down the street. But now the situation has changed, and it's getting harder and harder to get a loan.

The other day a man I know walked into a bank in Washington and said to one of the assistant vice-presidents, "Hello, friend."

"I'm not your friend," the vice-president said. "I have no friends."

"Don't you remember me?" the man said. "I was in here a year ago and wanted to borrow fifteen hundred dollars, and you said I could have three thousand because you liked the suit I was wearing."

"I remember," the VP said.

"And you told me anytime I wanted any money to just walk in with a satchel and I could have it. Remember?"

"I may have said it. So what?"

"Well, here I am back again, and I just thought I'd like to have about five thousand to tide me over for six months or so. I brought my satchel with me, hah, hah, hah."

"I couldn't give you five hundred. What's the matter? Do you think banks are made of money?"

"Well, you don't have to get sore."

"Don't tell me not to get sore. Why can't you live within your means like everyone else? That's all people ever think about these days, borrowing money. Haven't you ever heard of thrift?"

"Gosh, I'm sorry. I didn't realize that borrowing was wrong."

"Of course not. You just think anytime you run out of money, you can hop down to a bank with a satchel and say, 'Fill it up.' Well, mister, I've got news for you. We're wise to people like you. If you can't make a go of it on your income, we're not about to help you over the rough spots."

"But there's a big neon sign outside that says, 'We Make Loans Anytime Anywhere to Anybody.'"

"That doesn't mean you," the VP said.

"Look, I've got collateral. I could put up my house against the loan."

"Well, isn't that a nice thing to do? You'd risk your house and the welfare of your family for five thousand dollars. Don't you have any shame?"

"I hadn't thought of it that way," the man said. "I have a car. Would you take that?"

"We wouldn't even take the Ford plant in Dearborn for

five thousand dollars, if you want the truth. Now are you going to go quietly, or do you want to be arrested for disturbing the peace?"

"I just can't understand it. You *are* the same man I talked to a year ago, aren't you?"

"No banker is the same man you talked to a year ago," the VP said, wiping away a tear.

"Gee, I didn't mean to make you cry."

Now the VP was sobbing uncontrollably. "If you want to know the real reason you can't have a loan, it's that we don't have any money."

"That's awful," the man said. "Is there anything I can do?"

"Would you consider opening an account with us?"

"Why, sure, fellow," the man said, handing the VP his handkerchief. "And I want you people down here at the bank to know you always have a friend on Hawthorne Street."

E-E-E-E-KONOMICS

The three things that seem to disturb Americans are the Vietnam war, the racial unrest in the cities, and the status of the economy.

While the first two are very perplexing to the average person, the nation's economy is something everyone understands, particularly if one keeps abreast of the government pronouncements, as well as what our leading economists have to say. I was very fortunate at a cocktail party recently to run into an economist who was most reassuring about the future.

"You seem worried," he said kindly.

"I am," I admitted. "I'm worried about inflation."

"You have nothing to worry about. It's true that there is inflation at the moment, but you know, a little inflation isn't really a bad thing."

"It isn't?"

"I'm not saying it's a good thing," he said. "But when you have a booming economy, prices tend to rise. The important thing is to produce more. Yet the danger is that if you produce more, you have a shortage of labor and materials, which drives wages and prices up."

"Then it would be better if we had less employment and people didn't buy as much?"

"Not necessarily. If people buy less, you may have a recession problem, and while you don't want your economy to heat up too fast, you certainly wouldn't want it to cool off, would you?"

"Heck, no," I said. "I think it should be like wine and be kept at room temperature."

"Of course, there's the British pound," he said casually.

"What about the British pound?" I cried in alarm.

"It's waging quite a fight against devaluation."

"What's that got to do with us?"

"My dear fellow, it has absolutely everything to do with us. If they devalue the pound, do you think the dollar could defend itself?"

"I was hoping it could," I said honestly.

"Not without vast gold reserves. Unfortunately, our reserves are down, particularly since France has been cashing in her dollars."

"I knew France was behind all our troubles," I said.

"It isn't just France. The real problem seems to be our military commitments in Germany."

"I knew if it wasn't the French, it would be the Germans."

"I would say it wasn't the Germans as much as the American tourist. He's spending all our hard-earned dollars abroad."

"The dirty rat," I snarled.

"Yet I think we could weather all this if it weren't for the wage guidelines set up by the Administration."

"They're too low?"

"Not according to management. You see, management is caught in a profit squeeze. It isn't easy for them."

"Poor management."

"Yet labor does have a point in that the guidelines are unrealistic. You have to take into consideration the cost-of-living index when you talk about labor. Of course, if we had a tax increase, it might be another solution to our problems."

"I should hope so," I said gratefully.

"Would you like to hear my theory on why the price of bread has gone up again?" he asked.

"I wouldn't miss it for the world."

THE FANTASY WORLD OF MONOPOLY

The weather had not been the greatest on Cape Cod that year, and I found myself spending a great deal of time playing the game of Monopoly with my children. This battle for real estate has probably been the most popular pastime for children for more than three decades, and its appeal now is as great as it was when it first came out in 1935.

The surprising thing about Monopoly is that while inflation has taken its toll in this country, the prices for real estate on the Monopoly board have remained the same for thirty-three years. It's very hard for a parent to explain to his children how lucky they are that they can still purchase Marvin Gardens for only $280.

"In my day," I told my children, "two hundred and eighty dollars was a lot of money, and you thought twice about buying Marvin Gardens before you plunked down cash for it. Now the minute you land on it, you throw the money down as if it was water."

"Do you want to buy it, or don't you?" my thirteen-year-old son demanded.

"Don't rush me. If I buy Marvin Gardens, I'll have to buy Ventnor and Atlantic avenues, and they've really gone to seed in thirty years. I'll wind up with a bunch of tenements on my hands."

"Will you please roll the dice?"

"I'm just trying to impress on you the value of a dollar," I said. "Monopoly is more than a game. I don't want you kids growing up thinking you can buy the Pennsylvania Railroad for two hundred dollars. The Reading Railroad, maybe—but not the Pennsylvania."

"If you don't roll, you'll miss your turn."

"Now hear me out," I said. "You children must understand that every piece of real estate on this board is undervalued. When I was a child, we mortgaged everything just to own a piece of the Boardwalk. But today anybody can buy Boardwalk or Park Place. You kids don't appreciate Boardwalk and Park Place because you never had to work for them."

They pretended they didn't hear a word I said.

A dozen turns later I landed on "Chance." The card I

picked up said, "Go to jail. Do not pass Go. Do not collect $200."

"Wait a minute," I protested. "You can't just send a man to jail without charging him and advising him of his constitutional rights. Thirty years ago it could be done, but since then the Supreme Court has ruled that a man must be represented by a lawyer."

"You have to go to jail," my ten-year-old daughter said.

"I don't have to go to jail," I said. "Haven't you ever heard of the Mallory ruling or the Gideon case?"

My twelve-year-old plunked my token in jail and took her turn. She landed on "Income Tax: pay 10% or $200."

"That's ridiculous," I cried, looking at the stack of money in front of her. "You should be at least in the forty percent bracket. You own both the Water Works and the Electric Company. How do we pay for the war and the Great Society if you only contribute ten percent of your income?"

Once again my protests fell on deaf ears.

Two hours later, through some dirty trading, my children controlled everything on the board except Baltic and Mediterranean avenues, which I owned. Even thirty years ago they were considered slum areas, and I begged the children for urban renewal funds. But none of them would give me any money.

"All right," I said, "if you won't lend me money for urban renewal, would you at least give me twenty-five dollars for rat control?"

Once again they refused, and I decided that this was the only part of the game that had kept up with real life. When people own Illinois, Indiana, and Kentucky avenues, why should they give a darn what happens on Baltic and Mediterranean?

THE THIRD LARGEST INDUSTRY

One of the ways to solve acute problems in the United States is to study them. At this writing there are probably more committees making more studies of more problems than at any time in our history.

Professor Heinrich Applebaum has just completed a study on people who make studies, and the results are fascinating.

Professor Applebaum said, "I discovered that the average person making a study today has had 5 years of college, is married, has 1.6 children, earns $15,000 a year, lives in the suburbs, plays tennis or golf on weekends, and believes in God."

"That's truly amazing."

"He will spend an average 8.9 months working on a study, 2.6 months discussing it in committee, 3.9 months writing a report, which will be typed up by 5.6 secretaries, and then it will be printed up and distributed to 1,250 persons, who will read it in its entirety."

"That isn't too many people."

"It's a lot considering that only 1 out of every 23.6 reports is ever acted on."

"What happens to the rest of them?"

"They're filed away and used as reference for other people who will be asked to make future studies on the same subject."

"That sounds rather discouraging."

"On the contrary. The main purpose of a study is not to solve a problem, but to postpone the solution of it in the hope that it will go away. If it doesn't go away, at least people will have forgotten about it by the time the report comes out."

"Could you give me an example?"

"Well, at the moment the riots in Detroit are under study. A blue-ribbon panel of politicians appointed by the President is making a report, which will probably be delivered sometime in 1968. By then some other city will probably be burned down, and nobody will give a damn what happened in Detroit. They'll demand to know what happened in Philadelphia or Cleveland or whatever city blows up next. The President will then appoint another commission to study *that* riot, and by the time they get their report in, the President will have to appoint another committee to study what went wrong in Washington, D.C., or Oakland, California."

"A study group's work is never done."

"I should say not. Making studies is now the third largest industry in the United States. Not only are large monies spent in making studies, but great sums are also spent attacking studies that people don't agree with. Whenever the Public Health Service issues a report on smoking, the tobacco industry immediately attacks it with a study of its own."

"Even the National Guard doesn't like to be studied," I said.

"That's the beauty of the business. Every study demands a counterstudy to refute its facts."

"Professor Applebaum, your report will make a great contribution to the study of studies. Can you tell me why you decided to do it in the first place?"

"I work for a foundation, and everything we wanted to study was being studied by somebody else. This was the only subject left that no one had made a study on."

"Has anybody read it?"

"My wife thinks it's the best thing I've ever done."

8

�֎ �֎ ✖ ✖ ✖ ✖ ✖ ✖ ✖ ✖ ✖ ✖ ✖ ✖ ✖

NO DROPOUT, HE—

THE OTHER WAR

The operations room of the Twenty-fourth U.S. Army Recruiting Corps was tense with excitement. General Rubicom, the commanding officer, came in with his staff and stared at the map on the wall.

"Any news from the front, Colonel?"

"Yes, sir. We've heard from the Dartmouth patrol. They managed to get on campus unseen and got their card table set up in the administration building. They report they signed up four students for Officer Candidate School before they were discovered and had to retreat."

"Good show. Any word from Princeton?"

"No, sir. Not for two days. The last report we had was that Captain Reilly and his men were surrounded by students who wouldn't let their car move. They're running short on water and food, and I don't know how much longer they'll be able to hold out."

"Call the Air Force, and ask them if they'll make a drop."

"I did, sir; but the weather's been bad, and all planes are grounded."

"Dammit, Colonel, we have to get relief to them somehow."

"I know, sir. We were thinking of sending in a relief force, but we've used up all our reserves at Harvard."

"What's the situation at Harvard?"

"Lieutenant Shivers is trapped with three recruiters in the office of the *Harvard Crimson.*"

"Lieutenant Shivers?" a major cried. "That's my brother. How can you send a kid up to a place like that?"

"Easy does it, Major," General Rubicom said grimly. "Lieutenant Shivers knew what he was doing when he volunteered for the Twenty-fourth U.S. Army Recruiting Corps."

"Sure, you can say that, standing here in this nice comfortable office seven stories underneath the Pentagon. But what about the kids you send out day after day to Ohio State and the universities of Michigan, Wisconsin, and California at Berkeley? What are you running, a suicide mission?"

"Major, I will overlook your insubordination because I know how you feel about your brother. But I would just like

114

to assure you that I'm not heartless. How do you think I feel every time I send a patrol out to Yale or Columbia or Oberlin? Sure, I know they may never come back. But we've got a job to do, and I can't let emotion stand in the way of the Army's recruiting plans. Somebody's got to do the dirty work. War is hell, son."

At this juncture, the colonel said, "Sir, we've just got word from Reilly at Princeton."

"What does he say?"

"His message reads: 'Send us more students.' "

The general smiled. "Isn't that typical of Reilly, Colonel? I want to recommend him for the Distinguished Recruiting Cross, and send out that quote to the press. We need a hero at a time like this."

"Sir, the First Provisional Recruiters Brigade has just got back from Stanford," a staff officer said.

"How many missing?"

"Five. Schwartz, Weatherill, Puchinski, Kelly, and Ascereiil were last seen going into the student union to rescue a Dow Chemical Company recruiter, and they never came out."

The general looked off into space and said, "Why do the good ones always go first?"

NO DROPOUT, HE—

It is probably a very unfair thing to say, but many students are staying in college these days to avoid the draft. No one will admit it, but these students will take any subject if it means staying out of the Army.

I discovered this one day when I was on the campus of one of our larger universities and started talking to a student in the cafeteria.

He said, "I think it's very important that America have educated students, and while I'm willing to do my service as well as the next person, I think I will be able to serve my country better if I have a well-rounded education."

"How old are you, sir?"

"I'm fifty-one years old."

"But when did you start going to college?"

"In 1942, the semester right after Pearl Harbor. I felt we

were going to be in a long war with the Japanese, and there would be a big demand for college graduates. So I got a deferment and studied premedicine. But after four years I switched my major to agriculture because I decided what America would really need was farmers. I studied farming for three years and then switched to law because I heard there was a shortage of lawyers in the armed forces.

"But apparently I was misinformed, so I then decided to study chemical engineering."

"And all this time you were deferred from military service?"

"Yes. I would have gone anytime they asked me, but my draft board was very kind about it, especially when I explained my only reason for staying in college was to become a teacher.

"Of course, when Korea started, I was in a bad position, so I went to see my faculty adviser, and he told me I ought to study to become a veterinarian as the Army was short of veterinarians, and they would defer me for that. I studied to be a veterinarian during most of the Korean war, but then the Army announced it had too many veterinarians, so I switched to architecture."

"You've really had a well-rounded education," I said.

"I think I've gotten a lot out of school," he said, "though sometimes my father complains about my tuition. In the last twenty-six years it cost him sixty-seven thousand, four hundred and five dollars in tuition fees, not counting what it costs at my fraternity house and to take girls out. But my mother says she would still rather have me in college than in the service."

"And she's right," I said. "What are you taking now?"

"Well, I seem to have taken every course in the school, so I'm taking premed again."

"Have you ever gotten a degree in anything?"

"Oh, no. I've thought about it many times, but if I got one, I think it would take the fun out of college. Besides, if I got a degree, my draft board might not let me stay in school."

"Have you ever toyed with the idea of just giving up school sometime and taking a job?"

"I have once in a while. But I don't want people to say I'm a dropout."

"You've got a point. How much longer do you think you'll go to school?"

"I'm not sure. I was about to get out a few years ago, but then Vietnam came along, and my mother said I should stay, at least until I finished my education."

A SURVEY OF THE DRAFT

The draft law has been up for criticism, and there have been charges made that the present method of drafting our young men has been discriminatory and favors the rich and the smart.

I discussed this matter with several men to find out if they had any solution to the problem.

I asked one young man if he had any ideas on what would be the fairest way to draft Americans into the service.

"I think it should be done alphabetically," he said, "starting with the *A*'s and going right down the line."

"That's very interesting, sir," I said. "What is your name?"

"Uriah Zyckowski."

I stopped a man around forty on the street and asked him what he thought.

"I think it's wrong to take young boys who don't want to go," he said. "They should draft men who are married and have kids. They're the only ones who can appreciate what a good life the Army really is."

I walked over to a convertible a young man had just parked.

I asked him how he felt about the draft. "I don't believe they should draft men who own automobiles. We contribute too much to the economy of the country, and without a strong economy you can't have a strong defense system."

"Then you would defer all young men who own cars?"

"Yes, sir. It's unfair to take kids who have just found a good parking space."

I went over to a group that was demonstrating against the draft and sat down on the sidewalk with a bearded youth. "I presume you're against the draft."

"Heck, no, I'm for it."

"But you're against sending draftees to Vietnam?"

"I should say not. I think everyone should serve his country."

"Then why are you sitting on the sidewalk?"

He looked around and then whispered, "I'm with the FBI. Get the hell out of here."

I wandered over to the campus of American University.

A student said, "I think we should draft left-wingers, malcontents, and draft-card burners first. Those of us who believe in our country and will stand up for it as patriotic Americans should be allowed to finish our education."

"That makes sense," I said.

Another student said, "I'm with Secretary of Defense McNamara and I'm for his plan of having young people serve in something if they don't want to serve in the Army."

"What would you be willing to serve in?" I asked him.

"The Diners' Club."

One student said, "I'll go gladly if George Hamilton will go with me."

Another student said, "We ought to go back to the old British system of buying yourself out of the Army. This would make it profitable for the poor guys who have to go in, and it would salve the consciences of the rich guys who manage to stay out."

The final student I talked to said, "I think if you're old enough to drink, you're old enough to serve in the Army."

"That's a very courageous statement. What's your draft status?"

"I'm 4-F because I'm a chronic alcoholic."

HOW HAMILTON PERSUADED CARMICHAEL

It was just coincidence that movie actor George Hamilton and black power leader Stokely Carmichael were notified on the same day that they were up for draft reclassification. The reaction of the news varied as far as the two men were concerned. Hamilton said if his country needed him, he would be happy to serve, while Carmichael said he'd rather go to Leavenworth Prison.

Wouldn't it be wonderful if Hamilton could persuade Carmichael to go into the Army?

I can see the scene now. Hamilton is sitting on an Army bench waiting for his physical, and Carmichael is sitting next to him.

"Hello, my name's George Hamilton. What's yours?"

"Burn, baby, burn."

"Oh, you're Stokely Carmichael of the Student Non-Violent Coordinating Committee. I've seen you on television. Tell me, have you seen any of my movies?"

"Baby, I only go to movies where they don't let me in."

"Don't you think it's wonderful that they finally decided to classify us 1-A?" Hamilton says. "I've been trying to get in the Army for the last six years, but I'm the chief support of my mother, and my draft board insisted I take care of her first. I was naturally very disappointed, as I'd much rather be in the Army than be a civilian and live in a thirty-nine-room house in Hollywood."

"You may feel that way, baby, but I'm not going to be a black mercenary and fight a white man's war in Asia."

"I feel entirely differently about it," Hamilton replies. "The way I see it, there is a moment of truth in every man's life when you have to decide whether you'd rather make one hundred thousand a picture with Ursula Andress or Brigitte Bardot or fight for your country against Communism."

"Yeah, and which do you want to do?"

"Serve my country, of course."

"You're trying to get out on a psychiatric discharge, aren't you, baby?"

"You're being unfair. I'm looking forward to this experience. It will not only be enlightening, but I'm eagerly anticipating the training and the discipline of the Army, as well as the comradeship and *esprit de corps* that is so much a part of the military service."

"Man, you are a good actor, aren't you?"

"Stokely, you have no idea how awful it feels to know you're safe in a movie studio, making love to Sophia Loren, while out there our boys are giving their all to repulse godless aggression."

"I never thought about it in those terms before," Carmichael says.

"This may sound strange to you, but I'd rather wade through a rice paddy in the Mekong Delta than dance till three o'clock in the morning at the White House."

"Wouldn't we all, baby? Wouldn't we all?"

"I knew you'd see it my way, Stokely."

"I just hope I'm physically fit," Carmichael says excitedly, "because I'm raring to go."

Just then Cassius Clay walks in and sits down.

Stokely sticks out his hand. "My name's Carmichael, what's yours?"

"Burn, baby, burn," Clay says.

"That's the way I felt when I came in," Carmichael replies. "But then I got to talking to my buddy George. Hey, George, baby, here's another conscientious cat. Tell him what you told me."

IT ISN'T WHAT IT USED TO BE

Many students have been interviewed concerning how they felt to discover they were part of a CIA-financed operation, but nobody has bothered to interview anyone from the CIA to ask how he felt to be part of a student organization.

I had the good fortune to speak to a CIA man on a park bench in Lafayette Square. I knew he was a CIA man the minute I saw him because he was counting out $100,000 in cash to give to several students who were picketing the White House to stop the bombing in Vietnam.

One of the bills blew away, and when I retrieved it for the agent, he told me to keep it and invited me to sit down.

"It's very discouraging," he said. "Here I thought I had joined a professional outfit, and it turns out that all I'm doing is giving money to students and labor union leaders."

"But that's a big responsibility," I said. "Not everyone can be a James Bond."

"That's all right for you to say," he replied, feeding a squirrel a $100 bill. "But when I joined the CIA, I thought it was just a few of us fighting the evil forces of Communism throughout the world. Now it turns out every Tom, Dick, Harry, and even Gloria is working for the CIA. Half the damn country is somehow supported by the organization, and there just doesn't seem to be any distinction in being a secret agent anymore."

"It's true that there are more of you than you thought," I said. "But you have to remember it was your money that made the whole thing possible."

Just then a man came up and said, "I need seventy-five thousand to send a Vassar student tour up the Amazon."

The CIA agent counted out $75,000 and gave it to the man.

"May I have an extra five for lunch?" the man asked.

The agent gave him $20. "Everyone thinks we're made of money," he said to me after the man left. "But the truth is they're getting very sticky over at headquarters. You have to prove you're a completely independent organization without any possible government ties before you can become eligible for CIA funds."

"I guess there aren't many of those left anymore," I said.

"Well, all I can say is that I'm getting out of the organization. It has no status anymore. I was up for promotion the other day, and do you know who beat me out for it? One of the editors of the *Harvard Lampoon*."

A motorcycle roared up, and a tough, bearded fellow in a leather jacket came over. "We need twenty-five grand to start a chapter in Wilmington, Delaware."

The CIA man gave him $25,000.

"Are you behind the Hell's Angels, too?" I asked in amazement.

"Don't ask," the agent replied.

"I don't know how to say this," I said, "but I have a syndicated column, and I'm up to my ears in debt. I'm sure I could perform some service for you."

"How much do you need?" the agent asked.

"Could I have ten thousand dollars to start with? With that kind of money I could really fight Communism."

He reached into his satchel and counted out the cash. "Well, that about cleans me out," he said. "I'll have to go back to Langley and get some more."

"Thanks a million," I said gratefully.

"Don't mention it. We've been trying to put a columnist on the payroll for a long time now. Besides, you have an honest face."

9

※※※※※※※※※※※※※※※※

HEY, THERE!

THE FIRST SUPERSONIC FLIGHT

"Good day, ladies and gentlemen, this is your captain speaking, and I'm happy to announce that this is the first supersonic flight from New York to Paris. We will be flying at an altitude of sixty thousand feet and a speed of eighteen hundred miles an hour. Our flying time from New York to Paris will be two hours and forty-five minutes. Now please fasten your safety belts, and we will be ready to take off. . . .

"Ladies and gentlemen, I know you're wondering what the delay is, as we have been on the ground waiting to take off for the past two hours. Unfortunately, air traffic conditions are very heavy at this hour, and we have been asked to hold here on the runway. We are now the twentieth in line for takeoff. . . .

"Well, folks, we've been moving up, as you might have noticed, and we are now second in line. I'm sorry these last four hours have been so difficult, but the tower has assured us we will get clearance to take off in the next hour or so. . . .

"May I have your attention, please? It appears that there are more planes in the pattern than was expected, and we've been asked to hold further. Why don't you all relax? I've turned the No Smoking light off. . . .

"Ladies and gentlemen, we've finally been cleared for takeoff. Would you all please relax? I apologize for the six-hour delay at the runway, but this is something we have no control over. . . .

"Well, folks, we seem to have broken some sort of record. Our flying time to Paris was two hours and thirty-one minutes. Unfortunately, there are many planes circling the Orly Airport, and we've been asked to fly over to Copenhagen and hold there at fifty-five thousand feet. Paris assures us that as soon as it is feasibly possible, they will permit us to make an approach. . . .

"Ladies and gentlemen, this is your pilot speaking. Since I last spoke to you, ninety minutes ago, I regret we have not been encouraged by Paris to come in, and they have asked us to maintain altitude and fly in a pattern over Sicily.

"The stewardess tells me there seems to be a shortage of

drinks and water, so we are putting everyone on rations of one glass of water each.

"Also, I'm sorry to say we have run out of food.

"Some of you have complained about seeing the movie four times, so for the next two hours we'll play stereophonic music instead.

"You'll be kept informed about our progress. . . .

"Folks, this is the captain again. I know you're all very tired and hungry and thirsty, and so am I; but trying to knock down my door is not going to help anybody. We should be getting the green light from Paris any time now. . . .

"We've just heard from Paris, and we are now in the pattern and will be permitted to land within the next hour. Please fasten your safety belts. . . .

"This is your captain again. As you can gather, we are on the ground at Orly, France. Unfortunately, there doesn't seem to be any room at the ramp, and we've been asked to wait out here until someone leaves. It should not be more than forty or fifty minutes. . . .

"Well, here we are at the terminal, and I hope you've enjoyed your first supersonic flight. I'm happy to announce we beat the *Queen Mary*'s record by four hours and twelve minutes."

THE HUMAN ENGINEER

There is a new science in this country which is called human engineering. The object of human engineering, as I understand it, is to fit human beings into inhuman conditions.

I made this discovery while riding on an airplane from New York to Washington the other day. Seated next to me was a man who was taking very careful measurements of the space between us and then writing it in a notebook.

I asked him what he was doing, and he said he was a human engineer, and it was his job to see how many more people he could squeeze on an airplane without doing permanent bodily harm to the passengers.

"We used to have five seats across," he said proudly, "but we've managed to put another seat in each row, and as you can see, we can now get six people across."

"How on earth did you do it?" I asked him.

"We cut the center aisle in half. The passengers have to walk sideways, but just think of what the extra seats mean to the company's payload."

"Which, of course, is all that you're worried about?"

"You can bet your sweet whistle on that," he said. "I'm very concerned, though, that there still seems to be room between your knees and the seat in front of you."

"Only about two inches," I said.

"Well, if you take two inches away here and two inches away there, you can put another row of seats on the plane."

"Then my knees should be flush against the seat ahead?"

"Naturally, my dear boy. You can't expect legroom on such a short hop. One more thing. I was wondering how you feel about a reclining seat as opposed to a stationary one."

"I prefer a reclining seat. It gives me a chance to rest a little."

He started writing in his book: "Customer too tempted by reclining chair, so I strongly recommend stationary kind, which will allow us two more rows in back."

He looked at me. "You came on board with a package. What did you do with it?"

"I put it under my seat."

He wrote again, "Customer can still get package under seat, which means we're wasting valuable space which could better be used for airfreight."

"You people really think of everything," I said.

"We try to," he replied, "but it's a tough struggle. There are a lot of people in the aviation business who are behind the times, and we have to show them that their best interests lie not with the passengers but with the stockholders. I'm having a devil of a time trying to get the company to remove the armrests."

"You want to do away with the armrests?"

"Of course. If you did away with the armrests, everyone would be forced to sit closer together, and we could get eight people in a row."

"Say, have you ever thought of putting people in the baggage rack overhead?" I asked him.

He studied it for a few moments. "It could be done, if we could fit them in horizontally." He made another note: "Check about stuffing people into overhead baggage rack."

"You covered all the bases," I said in admiration.

"Not quite," he said, staring at the washroom.

A HAWK IN SPACE

The U.S. Senate was discussing a treaty on outer space with the Soviet Union which provides that the moon and other celestial bodies shall be used exclusively for peaceful purposes, and the establishment of military bases is prohibited.

Senator Eugene McCarthy of the Senate Foreign Relations Committee thinks we're getting our treaties all mixed up. If we're going to have a war, he would much prefer it to take place in outer space rather than in the populated areas where we seem to fight our battles now.

His suggestion is that we should be working on a treaty that says any future wars must be fought *only* in outer space, and the place where people live must be used *exclusively* for peaceful purposes.

There has been so much concentration on the troubles in Vietnam that we haven't been able to devote much thought to outer space. I personally think it would be a great mistake to use outer space for peaceful purposes. This is not only because of Senator McCarthy's remarks but because if we go exploring other celestial bodies without a military capability, we're bound to get into a heck of a lot of trouble.

The moon, as far as anyone can tell, is no problem, but once you start messing around with other planets, you're bound to run into hostile situations.

We have to assume there is life in outer space, and we also have to assume these beings are not necessarily going to welcome us with open arms. If they're smaller than we are, they will be afraid that we have come to conquer them. And if they're larger than we are, they'll probably beat us up, just for the fun of it.

At the beginning we might be able to get along with them, but pretty soon as more people arrive from earth, there's bound to be friction. It might start over a simple thing like a girl (or whatever they call them in outer space), or it could be caused by our building a liquor store on a planet and not selling the natives any drinks because of their color (we'll have to figure they're going to be green until we hear otherwise), or it could begin because we promised to pay them twenty-four dollars for their planet and then reneged on it.

In any case, the first settlers from earth will have to have protection from space beings, and this would be the job of the U.S. Space Cavalry. They would build forts around our settlements, send out patrols along the Milky Way, and move the space beings to special reservations set up for them, presumably on uninhabited planets. If the beings refused to go, the cavalry would have no choice but to attack and destroy them.

Another reason for not signing the treaty is that if we visited other planets, their beings might demand reciprocal rights to visit the earth, and J. Edgar Hoover and the FBI would be hard pressed to keep tabs on all of them.

There may be doves who say that the military should keep their hands off celestial bodies, but experience tells us that if we show any sign of weakness to other planets, they will interpret it as an indication that we're not willing to fight for what we believe in.

So I say, it's a mistake to approve a treaty on outer space, if it doesn't provide for adequate defensive measures against green spatial enemies, who would destroy any way of life we might set up out there.

Write your Senator today.

A FLYING SAUCER EXPERT

Every time I go out lecturing, I discover that one of the first questions that comes up is, "Do you believe in flying saucers?"

I don't know why people are always asking me that question unless it's because I look like the type of person who might have seen one.

There has been a lot of nonsense written about flying saucers, and it is for this reason that many people have reservations about them. The flying saucer business has become a multimillion-dollar industry, and any book on the subject will sell in the hundreds of thousands. Some of these books are pure nonsense, but others are so well written and documented that it gives one pause to think.

The most authoritative book to date on flying saucers has been written by Dr. Stegle Steglehofer and is titled *The Flying Saucer Cookbook*. Not only does Professor Steglehofer go into details on the flying saucers that he has seen, but he has also managed to gather together the favorite recipes of the captains of flying saucer ships.

The professor was in Washington to testify on the Truth in Packaging Bill and agreed to see me in his hotel suite.

"Professor, do you believe there are flying saucers?"

He was about to reply when he suddenly rushed to the window. "What was that?"

"What was what?"

"I thought I saw something strange fly by my windows."

"In Washington, D.C.?" I asked incredulously.

"Oh, they're getting more audacious all the time. Besides, they now know where the money is."

"What do you mean?"

"Well, the Air Force has just authorized three hundred and fifty thousand dollars to make a study of flying saucers, and the people on the saucers think they should have a say in how the money is spent. After all, it does affect them."

"That's true," I admitted. "So you believe they're liable to show up here?"

"I'm not making any predictions, but if they can convince Congress they exist, there is no telling how much money will be allotted to investigate them."

"How many flying saucers have you seen personally, Professor?"

"About thirty-three or thirty-four."

"Did you talk to any of the crew?"

"Only to the officers. I never talk to enlisted men."

"What did they say?"

"They're flying over the United States for peaceful purposes, and they'll stop their overflights only if the American people are allowed to decide their own destiny. They say they don't want to inflict their system on ours, but they are committed to protect the United States against aggression from Mars."

"Then, they're not from Mars?"

"No, they're from Venus. The ones that have been spotted over the Soviet Union are from Mars."

"That certainly complicates the picture. Does France have any flying saucers?"

"Only little ones. But it gives them a sense of grandeur. We'd much prefer that the United States and the Soviet Union were the only countries where you could see flying saucers, and we were even willing to share our sightseeing with them, but De Gaulle insists the French people see their own. Now Red China is starting to see them, too. In a few years there'll be flying saucers everywhere."

"Thank you, Professor, for talking to me."

"It's my pleasure." He ran back to the window. "There they go again. Damn, I told them not to land in the Rose Garden of the White House. Now, Lady Bird is really going to be mad."

HEY, THERE!

Pacific Airlines has been waging a very unusual advertising campaign pointing up the fears people have about flying. With such attention getters as "Hey, there! You with the sweat in your palms," security blankets for the passengers, and painting their airplanes to look like railroad locomotives, Pacific hopes to attract passengers who don't like to fly. It's a very dangerous campaign that Pacific is waging, but if it succeeds, other industries might decide to try the same approach.

The advertising agencies are watching the Pacific advertisements with interest and already have their own ads on the drawing boards. For example, the automobile people may get into adverse advertising with this kind of ad:

"Hey, there! You with the beer can in your hand. Have you ever thought if you took our Rake X-321 out tonight, you might ram it into a tree?

"Sure you're afraid to drive with all those nuts on the highways, and you certainly have good reason. First of all, you're not even certain that your car is safe, and then you don't know if anyone else's car is safe. Frankly, the way they're building the roads these days, you'd probably be better off staying in the house.

"But this shouldn't prevent you from buying a Rake X-321. For one thing, it's fast—too damn fast, if you ask us—and this can really scare you, if you lost control. But power isn't the only thing you have to fear in a Rake X-321. It skids like mad around a turn and it's top-heavy to boot. Matter of fact, the only safety feature we have on the car is a St. Christopher's medal.

"So why not go out and see your Rake dealer today?"

Then there are the bathroom fixtures advertising people.

"Hey, there! You with the shampoo in your eyes. Has it ever occurred to you that more people have accidents in bathrooms than anywhere else in the house? Sure it's kind of scary—particularly when you lose the soap in the bottom of the tub or when you accidentally walk through the glass door of a shower. But what are you going to do?

"Gurgle Plumbing Fixtures will not pretend to you that it's safe to take a bath. We feel the more facts you know about getting into a tub, the less anxious you'll be. The odds of getting in and out of a bath without hurting yourself are about four to one, which are not bad considering there is so little to hold onto when you're sitting down. Then there's always the chance of getting scalded if you turn the wrong tap. You say it will never happen? You should see some of the mail we get from our customers.

"Gurgle doesn't have the answer to accidents in the bathroom. All we can do is provide the equipment to make the accidents possible. Write for our free booklet 'The Bathroom Is Not Safe at Any Speed.' "

And then there are the drug people.

"Hey, there! You with the pain in your tummy. I guess you've read that Litmus Stomach Powders are safe. Well, don't let anybody kid you. If you take the wrong dose, you could be sick for two days. Litmus has an active coating ingredient that works twice as fast as any other stomach powder, which could cause a lot of complications. The powders come wrapped individually in plastic, and if you don't pull the flap according to instructions, you'll cut your finger.

"Many people are afraid to take Litmus Stomach Powders.

"And they're not dumb people, either.

"But we would rather you know in advance what you're getting into. Tests show bicarbonate is as good as Litmus, and it only costs half the price."

And finally, there are the cigarette advertisers.

"Hey, there! You with that terrible cough in your throat. . . ."

IS THERE LIFE ON EARTH?

There was great excitement on the planet of Venus this week. For the first time Venusian scientists managed to land a satellite on the planet Earth, and it has been sending back signals, as well as photographs, ever since.

The satellite was directed into an area known as Manhattan (named after the great Venusian astronomer Professor Manhattan, who first discovered it with his telescope 200,000 light-years ago).

Because of excellent weather conditions and extremely strong signals, Venusian scientists were able to get valuable information on the feasibility of a manned flying saucer's landing on Earth. A press conference was held at the Venus Institute of Technology.

"We have come to the conclusion, based on last week's satellite landing," Professor Zog said, "that there is no life on Earth."

"How do you know this?" the science reporter of the Venus *Evening Star* asked.

"For one thing, Earths' surface in the area of Manhattan is composed of solid concrete, and nothing can grow there. For another, the atmosphere is filled with carbon monoxide and other deadly gases and nobody could possibly breathe this air and survive."

"What does this mean as far as our flying saucer program is concerned?"

"We shall have to take our own oxygen with us, which means a much heavier flying saucer than we originally planned."

"Are there any other hazards that you discovered in your studies?"

"Take a look at this photo. You see this dark black cloud hovering over the surface of Earth? We call this the Consolidated Edison Belt. We don't know what it is made of; but it could give us a lot of trouble, and we shall have to make further tests before we send a Venus being there.

"Over here you will notice what seems to be a river, but the satellite findings indicate it is polluted, and the water is unfit to drink. This means we shall have to carry our own water, which will add even greater weight to the saucer."

"Sir, what are all those tiny black spots on the photographs?"

"We're not certain. They seem to be metal particles that move along certain paths. They emit gases, make noises, and keep crashing into each other. There are so many of these paths and so many metal particles that it is impossible to land a flying saucer without being smashed by one."

"What are those stalagmite projections sticking up?"

"They're some type of granite formation that gives off light at night. Professor Glom has named them skyscrapers since they seem to be scraping the skies."

"If all you say is true, won't this set back the flying saucer program several years?"

"Yes, but we shall proceed as soon as the Grubstart gives us the added funds."

"Professor Zog, why are we spending billions and billions of Zilches to land a flying saucer on Earth when there is no life there?"

"Because if we Venusians can learn to breathe in an Earth atmosphere, then we can live anywhere."

10

�֍✧✧✧✧✧✧✧✧✧✧✧✧✧✧✧

KEEP THE FAITH, BABY

PEACE CORPS BACKLASH

Thailand recently announced that she would send Peace Corps volunteers to the United States as a reciprocal gesture for American Peace Corps volunteers dispatched to Thailand.

The announcement said that several projects, including the teaching of the Thai language to Americans, would be worked out.

No one in his wildest dreams ever thought that there would be this kind of backlash to the Peace Corps. While the United States has been very eager to send Peace Corps volunteers abroad, we're not too certain it's such a great idea to have other countries send Peace Corps volunteers to the United States.

I can just see the first Thai Peace Corps volunteer, after spending two years in the United States, returning to Thailand and being interviewed by a newscaster on Bangkok television.

"We have in our studio Mr. Yok Bin Lin, who has just returned after serving two years in the United States as a Peace Corps volunteer. Mr. Lin, how was it over there?"

"I had a wonderful time, and I think I taught them a lot. The village where I worked in New Jersey was called Hoboken. By our standards it was very primitive, but the people were simple and friendly and willing to learn."

"Was it dangerous, Mr. Lin?"

"Well, you couldn't go out at night, but in the daytime it was perfectly safe to wander in most areas."

"Where did you live?"

"As you know, Thai Peace Corps volunteers are trained to live with the natives, so I moved into an urban housing development. It was hard at first, because the plumbing kept me awake at night, but after a while I got used to it."

"Did you eat the native food?"

"I tried to, but it wasn't easy. The Hoboken people refuse to raise any food themselves, and they must buy it at supermarkets frozen and wrapped in cellophane."

"You must be joking?"

"No, I'm not. One of my first projects was to try to teach the natives how to grow their own vegetables, so they

136

wouldn't have to spend money, but they were too set in their ways."

"What did you find was the Americans' biggest problem?"

"They're full of fears. It's very hard to work with the people because in the world they live in they've lived with fear for so long."

"What do you think the origin of the fear is?"

"It starts with their young, who are told at a very early age that they have bad breath, that they perspire too much, that they will probably get cavities, that they are susceptible to headaches, neuralgia, and stomach acids. By the time the young grow up, they're frightened of everything."

"What about the family structure?"

"There is not too much to speak of. The children go off when they're quite young and have a great hostility toward their elders. The husbands and wives don't get along too well either, so there is quite a bit of friction right inside the family."

"Looking back over the two years, Mr. Lin, what do you consider was the greatest contribution you made?"

"I got everyone in Hoboken to practice birth control."

IF ADAM HAD BEEN HUMBLE

It had been said that the reason the House of Representatives treated Adam Clayton Powell so badly was that Powell refused to show any humility. How different everything would have been if the ex-Congressman (at least for the moment) had thrown himself on the mercy of the House and asked forgiveness!

"Adam Clayton Powell, please step forward."

"Yassuh, boss."

"It has been charged that you have insulted this body of lawmakers."

"Ah'm a sinner. Amen."

"That you put your wife on your payroll although she did no work and received no checks."

"Ah did the taxpayers wrong. Lordy Lord."

"That you, furthermore, used an airline credit card for personal trips to Florida for yourself and your beautiful secretary and that you spent in excess of forty thousand dollars of government money."

"Praised be the government and all its good works."

"Adam Clayton Powell, you have lived high on the hog for twenty years. Your absenteeism record is known to all of us, and your contempt-of-court citation in New York still hangs over your head."

"How could Ah have done it after the white folks have been so good to me?"

"This House cannot allow anyone to violate its rules, nor can it allow anyone to be guilty of unethical conduct, particularly if it gets in the newspapers."

"Ah have seen the light. May Ah be struck down during a filibuster if Ah sin once more."

"It isn't enough to say you're sorry, Adam. You must be made an example of, or every Congressman will be putting his wife on his payroll and taking his secretary to Bimini."

"Let me be punished; let the full force of this House crash down on my head; and then let me dwell in the House of Representatives forever and ever."

"Adam Clayton Powell, this body is impressed by your humility, and we want to do everything we can to make your punishment as light as possible."

"Ah beg to differ with you, suh, but Ah think Ah should get the full treatment. What Ah have done is unforgivable. If you show me mercy, then Ah will not feel Ah have been forgiven. You must purge me of my guilt, for only then will Ah be able to shave and look at mahself in the morning."

"What should we do with you, Adam?"

"Let me pick a bale of cotton, pick a bale a day."

"That would be too harsh."

"Ah could tote a barge and lift a bale and if Ah got a li'l drunk Ah could land in jail?"

"I don't think that would be constitutional."

"But you don't understan', suh. Mah heart is weary and Ah'm sick of tryin'. Ah'm tired of livin' and 'feared of dyin'."

"Sing it, Adam."

"But old man river, he just keeps rollin' along."

"As you can see, Adam, there isn't a dry eye in the House. We're going to let you take your seat, because we're a forgiving people in this body, and when we see a man as humble as you, we can only say, 'Go forth, brother, and sin no more.'"

"Thank you, boss. Ah'll jes go take mah seat in the back."

YOU CAN'T TRUST ANYONE

One of the worst things to come out of the Dodd censure hearings is that no one can trust the people working for him anymore. It will be recalled that all Senator Dodd's troubles started when four staff workers got mad at him and copied all his files, which they turned over to Drew Pearson and Jack Anderson. Since then everyone in Washington has been watching the people who work for them like hawks.

I even found myself caught up in the hysteria.

The day after Senator Dodd was censured, I walked into my office and found my secretary, Elaine, going through the files.

"What are you doing in those files?" I screamed.

Elaine jumped. "I was just trying to get them into some kind of order. They're a mess."

"A likely story," I said. "You weren't going to have them copied and turned over to Drew Pearson, were you?"

"Why? Did you want me to?" she asked.

"Don't act innocent," I said. "How do I know I can trust you?"

"I've been working for you for four years," she said. "Have I ever given you any reason to doubt it?"

"That's not the point. You know what's in those files, and I know what's in those files. But if the public ever found out what was in those files, I wouldn't last in this town a week."

"That's what I've been telling you. If you'd just throw out all that stuff in your files, I'd have some room to work."

"Oh, no, I won't. That's my only protection. I have so many things in my files, you'd never be able to copy all of them."

"Why would I want to copy any of them? I want to throw them out," Elaine said angrily.

"Let me ask you a question," I said. "Suppose I fired you. What would you do then?"

"I'd get myself a decent job," she said.

"Oh, would you now? Or would you come back at night and Xerox everything in this office?"

"Why do you keep talking about firing me?" Elaine asked, almost in tears.

"Because you know too much. Remember that time Gregory Peck took me to lunch and I said I took him to lunch?"

"What about it?"

"It was a clear case of double billing, and you're the only one who knows about it. How would you like to be in the position of having somebody hang that over your head?"

"I just put down what you told me to put down," she said.

"That's what Michael O'Hare said Senator Dodd told him to put down. How do I know that someday you won't report that I used money given to me by Blue Cross to fix up my house?"

"You never did that."

"But it's your word against mine."

"I've got a lot of mail to be answered, so if you're finished, I'll get back to it," Elaine said.

"Sure, and don't forget to send a copy to Jack Anderson, while you're at it."

"Is that all?" she said, gritting her teeth.

"No, there's one thing more. Get me Senator Russell Long on the phone. I might as well be defended by the best man in town."

"BURN, BELSKY, BURN"

It is incumbent for every white man in these enlightened times to have a Negro friend, but it is very dangerous for a Negro to have a white friend.

Take my friend Belsky, if you will. Belsky is in all sorts of trouble, none of it of his own doing.

Belsky complained to me the other day, "You are looking at a man without a country. I am in hot water up to my ears, and I don't know what to do about it."

"How so, Belsky?" I inquired.

"Well, I did everything they told me to do. They said, 'Belsky, get an education, and you'll be able to throw off the chains of slavery and injustice that your people have suffered for nigh on three hundred years.' So I went out and got a college education. Then they said, 'Belsky, move out of the ghetto into a decent neighborhood, so your kids can breathe good air and grow straight and tall.' I moved out of the ghetto and found a nice home in a middle-class neighborhood, and everyone seemed happy that I had made it. The black people said, 'Look at old Belsky. He broke out of the neighborhood. If he can do it, we can, too.' And the white neighbors, after they got over the shock of it, said, 'You know, once you get to know Belsky, he's just like us.' I almost got the feeling they were proud to have me in the neighborhood.

"For three years everything was going along fine, and then one day a black relative said, 'Belsky's an Uncle Tom.' And another black friend said, 'Of course, he's an Uncle Tom. If he wasn't, he'd be living in the ghetto with us.'

"Another one said, 'Belsky has white friends. Anyone who has white friends must be Uncle Tomming it all the time.' And still another one said, 'His kids go to a good school. You know, he's sold out to whitey.' And so back in my old neighborhood everyone was saying, 'Burn, Belsky, burn.'

"I tried to point out I was only trying to do the right thing by integrating, but they said the only ones that want to integrate are Uncle Toms. Since I was a member of the PTA and had a good job with a company, it had to be assumed I was up to no good."

"You're in a tough spot," I had to admit.

"Well, that's just the half of it. I thought about it for some time and decided there was no sense moving back to the old neighborhood, and if the price of giving my kids a decent break was being called an Uncle Tom, I could live with it.

"But I hadn't reckoned with the effect the black power scare would have on the white people. Lately my neighbors have become very nervous. 'You want to burn down my house, don't you, Belsky?' one of them said. I denied it. 'Well, your people want to burn my house.' I denied my people wanted to burn down his house. 'Well,' he said angrily, 'someone wants to burn down my house.'

"Another neighbor said, 'Belsky, I'm wise to you and your black power, and I want you to know I've bought a gun.' Several kids, white kids, have been running by my house lately, shouting, 'Burn, Belsky, burn.' "

"Then, you're considered an Uncle Tom by the Negroes and a black power advocate by the white people?" I said.

"Exactly. Nobody's very happy with me, and everyone wants me to burn."

"Well, I want you to know, Belsky," I assured him, "you're still my friend, and if you want to, you can burn down *my* house anytime."

"Thanks," he said gratefully. "There aren't many people left like you anymore."

GHETTO, INC.

A friend of mine has just thought of a way to raise a large sum of money for poverty-stricken areas without one cent's cost to the taxpayer. He calls his program Ghetto Inc., and this is his explanation of how it works.

"From now until the Presidential elections in 1968," my friend said, "ghettos are going to be the big thing, and every politician running for public office is going to have to visit one. But most politicians don't know where to begin when it comes to touring the slums, and so Ghetto Inc. will make all the arrangements for them, for a fee, of course."

"What will you do?"

"Well, let us suppose the person wishing to tour a ghetto area is one of the many thousands of Presidential candidates who feel obligated to walk through a depressed area. Ghetto Inc. would make out an itinerary for him. First, we'd have him visit a rat-infested tenement, where he could be visibly shocked.

"Then we'd take him over to meet the parish priest who has just coached a Little League team of deprived youngsters to a city championship. After that we'd have him talk to an ex-convict who has gone straight and become a Good Humor man.

"Finally, we would arrange an interview with an unwed mother who has just lost her welfare payments. The candidate could or could not promise the woman he'd do something about it, depending on how he thinks the country feels at the time about unwed mothers."

"It sounds like a great service," I said. "How much does it cost?"

"Well, that's just a simple tour, and with transportation and including the ex-convict and Good Humor truck, we charge fifteen hundred dollars."

"That's not expensive," I said.

"Of course, Ghetto Inc. has more luxurious tours. We can arrange for a candidate to walk through a garbage dump, have him photographed with a group of striking schoolteachers, let him cut the ribbon for a new playground, and then lay the cornerstone for a low-cost housing development. The charge for this would be ten thousand dollars, and we'd supply the striking schoolteachers."

"You must be swamped with business," I said.

"Well, it's picking up nicely," my friend said. "Of course, the beauty of Ghetto Inc. is that we can service all candidates whether they're for or against the poverty program."

"How's that?"

"Suppose you have a candidate who is against welfare, opposed to coddling the poor and feels everyone should lift himself up by his own bootstraps."

"I know one," I said.

"Well, for twenty-five thousand dollars we'll arrange a tour for him which will include having rotten vegetables and eggs thrown at him, having paint spilled on his car, and, if he requests it, having the press roughed up. This will get him the sympathy of the backlash crowd, which he is appealing to in the first place."

"I could see a candidate asking for that kind of treatment, but where do you find the people to throw the rotten eggs and vegetables?"

"Oh, they're around; they're around."

"Well, I think it's a very noble experiment, and I can't see how Ghetto Inc. can miss," I said.

"It can't. As a matter of fact, with so many people running for office in 1968, our only fear is that we may run out of ghettos—or, even worse, unwed mothers—before the campaign is over."

UNCLE JOHN'S CABIN

The New Left held a meeting in Chicago and set back radicalism by twenty years. The original idea of the meeting was for it to help unite all the left-wing organizations under one banner and start a third party to defeat President Johnson in 1968.

But before anyone realized what was happening, a minority of militant black power delegates took over the conference, and the majority of white delegates found themselves giving in to every demand made of them by the likes of Rap Brown, Floyd McKissick, and James Foreman.

The black power people told the white delegates either to see every issue the Negro's way, "or they could go to hell." Instead of fighting back, the white leftists caved in and adopted every black power proposal from the boycotting of General Motors to condemning Israel for fighting a war against the Arabs in the Middle East.

This seems to be a reverse form of Uncle Tomism, and many of the white radicals are now being called Uncle Johns, because of their kowtowing to the militant Negro leaders.

It's a pitiable sight to see.

"Honkie," the black man says, "do you know who the worst enemies of the black people are?"

"We are, boss, the white liberals."

"And do you know why?"

"Oh, I wish I did. I wish I did."

"Because you're always trying to understand us. Can't you get it through your dumb head that we don't want to be understood?"

"You've got to give us time. That's all we ask for."

"It's too late, boy. The only thing we can do with you now is to burn down your house."

"I was going to suggest that myself. But I want to do more for you than that. Could I take you to lunch?"

"I can't afford to be seen having lunch with you, boy. I've got my reputation to think of."

"Of course you do. I'm sorry for getting out of line. I should know my place by now. What can I do to show my devotion?"

"Well, we really don't give a damn one way or the other, but if you want to get involved, you can support our program."

"Of course I will. What is it?"

"Impeachment of the President, free guns in the ghettos, the abolition of the Supreme Court, and the overthrow of the U.S. Government."

"There's nothing in there I couldn't support."

"But let's get something straight, boy. This is our show. We don't want you stealing it away from us."

"I wouldn't do that, sir. Say, if you won't have lunch with me, would you consider breakfast?"

"It's too risky, boy. I like you personally, but if I'm seen with you, I'd never be able to explain it to my people. You understand, don't you?"

"I do. I do."

"As a matter of fact, I shouldn't even be talking to you."

"Please don't reject me. The only thing I can't take is rejection."

"Get off your knees, boy. You're embarrassing me."

"I've still got this other shoe to do."

"Well, hurry up and finish the shine. I've got to go back into the meeting."

THE ANATOMY OF A LEADER

Negro "leaders" aren't born these days, but made—and in most instances by the news media.

Take the case of Robert Runneymeade as an example. Robert Runneymeade has been standing on the corner of Spring and Maple for the past three years (except when he's been in jail), saying to three or four hangers-on, "We ought to shake someone up." Nobody ever paid much attention to Robert Runneymeade until a few months ago, when a reporter for a local newspaper, doing a story on violence in the ghettos, happened to overhear Runneymeade saying to his friends, "Man, we ought to burn down this town."

The next day a story appeared in the paper that "Robert Runneymeade, a leader of the black power movement, told a militant crowd at Spring and Maple that it was time to burn down the town."

A television crew was dispatched the next evening to Spring and Maple, where his pals were congratulating Runneymeade on having made the front pages of the newspaper. The TV commentator stuck a microphone in front of Robert Runneymeade's face, lights were turned on, and for the next twenty minutes Runneymeade said, "The mayor, the city council, the honkies, and President Johnson have to talk to me."

The opposition television station sent out its camera crews to get the views of Runneymeade, and with all the lights and trucks a large crowd gathered, as they will when they see TV cameras.

The news media claimed that the crowd who had gathered were all Runneymeade's followers, when in fact most of them had never heard of Runneymeade, and those who knew him thought he was a joke.

But the press was not too interested in how many followers Runneymeade really had. He was now talking about burning down the Yosemite National Park, and this certainly had news value.

In the meantime, the networks had plugged into Runneymeade and he started holding press conferences telling everyone, "I'm not going to take any stuff from anyone, and if I have to wipe out the U.S. Marine Corps, I'm going to do it."

The Negro people still considered Runneymeade a joke, but the white people were scared out of their wits by his television appearances and his statements in the press. Things got so bad that when the President of the United States went on television to talk about the riots, his statement was played on the bottom of the page, and a statement made by Runneymeade threatening to use tanks against the public library was given a six-column headline.

It got so bad that no matter what happened, Runneymeade was the first interviewed about what his opinion was on the issues of the day. Runneymeade was quoted on Red China, Vietnam, the Middle East crisis. He appeared on the covers of both leading news magazines. The majority of the Negro community kept insisting that Runneymeade did not speak for them, but no one could make a headline or a TV news story out of that.

Unfortunately, the publicity had gone to Runneymeade's head, and one day he announced he was banning all white newspapermen from his press conferences.

Since they couldn't cover him anymore, the news media sought out another "Negro leader" on the corner of Marble and Sycamore streets. His name was Huggins Haplap, and he was overheard by a reporter the other day saying to a girl he was trying to impress, "I'm going to burn down the Grand Coulee Dam." It shouldn't be long before Haplap becomes a feared American name.

FRANCOIS WRITES TO PIERRE

Pierre Bernheim
16 Avenue Hoche
Paris, France

MY DEAR PIERRE,

Forgive me for not writing sooner; but as you know, there is a war going on in the United States, and I have been in my fallout shelter for several months.

Without giving away secrets, here is the military situation in the United States at the moment:

The Pentagon is still in the hands of the government. An assault last weekend by members of the Fifty-first Light Peace Brigade, known as the Fighting Doves, supported by the Thirty-third Flower Battalion, failed and was repulsed by members of the Eighty-second Airborne Division of the U.S. Army. There was heavy fighting in the north parking lot, and suicide units of the SDS (Students for a Democratic Society) managed to get to the steps of the building before they were turned back.

General Norman Mailer of the Twenty-second Heavy Obscenity Corps was captured, as were 600 other Militant Peace Commandos.

The attack started with a barrage of curse words, followed by an assault across the demilitarized zone with clubs, pop bottles, and tomatoes.

In fierce hand-to-hand combat the loyal government troops held their ground, and by evening Army spokesmen were able to announce that the Pentagon was safe, at least for the moment.

But while it turned out to be a military victory for the government, neutral observers here believe that President Johnson's pacification program in the United States is failing.

In order to win the war in the United States, Mr. Johnson has to win the hearts and minds of the American people. This he is failing to do, and there is considerable speculation that his regime may be overthrown by November 1968.

While the President still has support in Washington, D.C. (his wife, Senator Everett Dirksen, and his son-in-law), it's very hard to find it in the countryside. There has been fighting in Madison, Wisconsin; Boston, Massachusetts; Oakland, California; and Brooklyn, New York.

The military is dissatisfied with the civilian control of the situation and would like to wipe out the peace resisters once and for all. They want to bomb Harvard, Yale, the University of Michigan, the University of Wisconsin, and the University of California at Berkeley, but these targets, for political reasons, are still off limits.

The military men claim they can't win the war if the peace marchers continue to use the Dr. Benjamin Spock Trail.

So you see, my dear Pierre, the situation in the United States is quite serious, and some experts predict it will go on for twenty years. I know you are worried for our safety, but please be assured we are taking all precautions.

We sleep in the fallout shelter, and Hélène goes out only in the morning to buy bread and milk. I fly the French flag from my automobile to show everyone I am neutral, and if worse comes to worst, the embassy has assured us a cruiser will be sent to evacuate us. Thank God I kept my French passport.

Your *cher ami*,
FRANÇOIS

11

✕✕✕✕✕✕✕✕✕✕✕✕✕✕✕✕

WILL THE REAL MAO
PLEASE STAND UP?

WILL THE REAL MAO PLEASE STAND UP?

One of the most perplexing things about the situation in Communist China is that Liu Shao-chi is still walking around free in Peking. For those who haven't kept up with the events of the past year, Liu Shao-chi, as Chairman of the People's Republic, is China's chief of state. But ever since the Cultural Revolution began, he is the most reviled man in the government.

A day doesn't go by when he isn't attacked in the press or on wall posters or by the Red Guards. He has been accused by the Maoists of taking the capitalist road, of being a lackey of the Soviet Union, and of being in cahoots with Chiang Kai-shek. This is not to mention his other unspeakable crimes, such as revisionism, imperialism, and bad breath.

Yet Liu is still for all intents and purposes the head of the Chinese government. How does he get away with it?

The only thing one can surmise is that Liu has something on Mao, and if he ever blows the whistle, Mao is going to wind up in bird's-nest soup.

China watchers have been speculating about what it could possibly be, and here are some of the theories they have come up with:

Mao owns the only television station in Canton. If he makes any attempt to kick out Liu Shao-chi, who controls the Chinese equivalent of the FCC, Liu will issue another license so there will be two TV stations in Canton. Mao's station could never stand the competition. And his TV interests, which are now in trust, would lose a fortune.

Another theory is that in order to launch his Cultural Revolution, Mao accepted money from the CIA. Liu found out about this when he discovered that the Hate America Every Day Foundation was really a conduit for CIA funds. Liu has warned Mao that if he makes any move against him, he will give the story to *Ram Pahs* magazine, and every student in China will turn against him.

Still another theory on why Liu has managed to survive is that he has proof that the *Thoughts of Mao* was ghostwritten by a professor at Shanghai University and that Mao hasn't

150

had an original thought since he became head of the Communist Party in China.

There are some China experts who believe that if you look behind the scenes, you'll find a woman. They say Mao has been having an affair with a Red Guard sorority mother, and Liu knows about it. Since the present Mrs. Mao is said to be an insanely jealous woman, Mao's life wouldn't be worth two chopsticks if she ever found out about it.

Another theory is that Mao is a compulsive gambler and has lost over two billion fens to Liu at fan-tan. The only way Mao could ever hope to get even is by keeping Liu alive and playing him double or nothing.

But the most interesting idea that has been put forth so far is that Mao and Liu are the same person. One night he sneaks out and puts up a poster against Liu, and the next night he sneaks out and puts a poster up attacking Mao. In that way, no matter who wins the Cultural Revolution, Mao or Liu will still be on top.

This final theory makes the most sense, though there are still some questions that have to be answered. If Mao is Liu and Liu is Mao, can Chou be far behind?

THE UNCOMMITTED COUNTRY

One of the most surprising stories in some time has to do with the tiny island of Anguilla in the Caribbean. It seems that Anguilla, with a population of six thousand, declared its independence from the island of St. Kitts and asked the United States for help in defending itself against Kittian government.

Without hesitation, the United States alerted the fleet, ammunition was loaded on planes, a Marine regiment was put on landing barges, and the great war machine of the United States was ready to go into action.

But then someone in the State Department discovered that the United States had no commitment to go to the aid of Anguilla in case of trouble.

"But that's impossible," the White House said. "The United States has commitments all over the world. Surely it has a commitment to Anguilla."

The State Department searched and searched and couldn't

come up with any paper ever signed between Anguilla and the United States.

"Perhaps," the State Department told the White House, "an American President made a commitment to Anguilla without telling us about it."

Since Anguilla is three hundred years old, the White House went through the private papers of every President from George Washington to Lyndon B. Johnson but was unable to find a mention of Anguilla in any of them.

A meeting of the National Security Council was called, and the President spoke his mind in no uncertain terms.

"Can someone explain to me why the United States has no commitment to go to the aid of Anguilla?"

The Secretary of State replied, "It was probably an oversight on the part of the previous administrations. We were so sure that another President had got us committed in Anguilla that we didn't bother to make a commitment to Anguilla, but when I looked it up, it turned out he made it to Antigua."

The President said, "Well, how can we go to the aid of Anguilla if no one has made a commitment to them?"

The Secretary of Defense said, "I don't think we can. We have no legal basis for it."

The President said, "I thought as much. The United States is pledged to honor its commitments throughout the world, and here we have a situation where we can't honor a commitment because we didn't make one in the first place. How will that make us look in the eyes of the Russians?"

The head of the CIA said, "Couldn't we make up a commitment to Anguilla and sign Abraham Lincoln's name to it? We have this special paper that we can age so no one will know the difference."

The U.S. Information Agency Director said, "It's dangerous. If someone could prove it was a forged commitment, all our other commitments around the world would be suspect."

The President said, "Leonard's right. I could never look Kosygin in the eye again if I knew I had a false commitment to Anguilla."

The Chief of the Joint Chiefs of Staff said, "Do you want us to scrub the operation?"

The President said, "I'm afraid we have no choice."

"What should we do with all the stuff?" the Secretary of Defense asked.

The President said, "Well, as long as it's all loaded, you might as well send it to the Congo."

THE CHINA WATCHER

It isn't easy to be a China watcher these days. Not only do you have to watch what is going on there, but you also have to interpret the significance of the events instantly.

I went over to see a China watcher friend of mine at the State Department. He was bleary-eyed and looked as if he hadn't slept for several nights.

"Watching China isn't what it used to be," he said wearily. "All we had to do in the old days was read the Peking newspapers and see who was standing next to Mao Tse-tung; then we could take the rest of the afternoon off and play golf. But now being a China watcher is a seven-day-a-week job, and we still don't know if what we're watching is what is really happening there."

"Could you briefly sum up in your own words how you see the situation," I said.

"As far as I can tell, there seems to be some kind of power struggle going on between the antiparty Maoists and the anti-Mao partyists. It started with the purging of writers Wu Han and Kuo Mo-jo and then went on to party bosses Teng Ho and Li Chi. After that they took off on Peng Chen and Lu Ting-yi, and Li Hsueh Feng, not to mention Chou En-lai."

"Who did?"

"Lin Piao, Li Chin, and Mrs. Mao."

"I always suspected they were up to no good," I said.

"Did I tell you about Liu Shao-chi?" he asked.

"I can't remember."

"Well, he was replaced by Lin Piao as Mao's heir apparent and denounced by Tao Chu. This was followed by Peng Teh-huai's arrest, and it didn't do Marshal Ho Lung any good, either."

"But why?" I demanded.

"Because, obviously, they were thinking un-Mao thoughts. You must try to understand that there is a power struggle going on between those who think Mao and those who don't think Mao. We think the leader of the Think Mao school is Ching."

"Who's he?"

"It's not a he; it's a she. Chiang Ching is the maiden name of Mrs. Mao Tse-tung. She seems to be running the show with Chen Po-ta."

"Who is she?"

"Chen Po-ta is a he, and he was responsible for the imprisonment of Chou Yang."

"Poor Chou Yang," I said. "He deserved better than that. Let me ask you something. Whose side are we on?"

"Of course," he replied, "we're always anti-Mao, but at the same time it would be premature to be pro-Liu, Tao Peng, Teng, Feng, and Ping."

"How about Chou?"

"I wouldn't trust him as far as I could throw Chen."

"You're down on Chen?"

"As far as I'm concerned, Chen and Ching are the same thing."

"I'm glad I talked to you," I said. "You certainly cleared up everything for me."

"Don't mention it. The one trouble with watching Red Chinese politics is that you think you've had your fill of it, but an hour later you're hungry again."

"OUR FRIENDS, THE RUSSIANS"

Red China is making threatening noises at the Soviet Union and has even said that if the Russians keep beating up Chinese students at Red Square, the People's Army of China will have no choice but to attack the Soviets in force.

American sympathies for the first time in years are with the Soviet Union, and while it's hard to believe, we may soon be referring to the Russians as "our valiant allies" again.

No one speaks about it, but there is a contingency plan for just such an eventuality, and it's headed by a State Department type named Horace Turnover.

I found Turnover in the subbasement of a temporary World War II building, located behind a door marked Department of Friendly Soviet-American Relations and Coordinating Commission.

When I walked in, I found him on his hands and knees, putting the last touches on a sign which said, "Take a Russian to Lunch."

Turnover seemed elated with the turn of events and said,

"For twenty-two years they made fun of me, but they aren't laughing anymore. Why, if things keep going as they are between the Soviets and the Red Chinese, they might even move me back to the State Department Building."

I noticed for the first time that Turnover's window was broken, and the snow was pouring in.

"I gather up until now they haven't given your department too much money."

Turnover pulled his overcoat collar tight around his throat. "You can say that again. You might even say they've tried to keep my department under wraps, but now all these years of waiting have paid off."

"What do you plan to do first?"

He took me over to a rusty metal cabinet and opened it.

"I have all the films here that we made about our valiant Russian allies during World War II: *Song of Russia, Convoy to Murmansk, The Meeting at the Elbe,* and *Our Friends, the Ukrainians.* As soon as I get the word, we're releasing them for television on the *Late Late Show.*"

"It will be nice to see them again," I said to him.

"Then we'll give the Soviets fifty old American destroyers as part of a new lend-lease program."

"But what do they need with destroyers? The Red Chinese have no Navy to speak of."

"It will be a friendly gesture. After that, we can send them the hard stuff. We'll explain to the American people that the Russians are fighting *our* war."

"Something like any attack on the Soviet Union is an attack on us?" I asked.

"Exactly. We might even bring over some Russian war heroes to sell U.S. defense bonds."

"Maybe we could have a rally in Hollywood for the Soviet Union Widows and Orphans Fund," I said excitedly.

"It's not going to be easy," Turnover said. "I called Hollywood and spoke to a writer about starting one, and he said the last time he organized such a rally, he couldn't find work for twenty-three years."

The snow was now blowing all over Turnover's desk.

"Well, I hope for your sake, the Red Chinese really give the Soviets a bad time," I said.

He replied, "I do, too. Otherwise, I'm going to be stuck with twenty crates of hammer and sickle buttons, and J. Edgar Hoover is sure to start asking questions about them soon."

THE MAN FROM UN

As the United Nations gets larger, its member countries are becoming smaller, and sometimes it's hard to recognize the name of a nation, much less to pronounce it. Not long ago I was in a restaurant in New York, and I got to talking to a man who turned out to be the ambassador to the United Nations from Boolah Boolah, a speck of land located somewhere between the Indian Ocean and the Antarctic Ocean.

"How many people in your country?" I asked him.

"I think about two thousand," he said. "I haven't been home for some time. My brother is the prime minister, and I'm the ambassador to the United Nations. We tossed a coin for our jobs, and he lost."

"Then you like being ambassador to the United Nations?"

"I adore it. The General Assembly is air-conditioned, we get diplomatic immunity when it comes to parking, and if you get tired of listening to the speeches, you can always tune in a transistor radio. Everyone thinks you're listening to the translation of a speaker."

"If you're such a small country, where do you get your funds to entertain?"

"I don't have to do any entertaining. Everyone wants to entertain me. First the Russians take me to lunch, then Americans take me to dinner, the Arabs have me over for shish kebab, and, I must say, they don't serve a bad breakfast at the Israeli delegation. If you get a good debate like this one, you can eat for months without picking up a check.

"The trick, of course, is never to tell them how you're going to vote. If you align yourself with one side or the other too early, you could starve to death."

"Then it's best to be neutral," I said.

"Absolutely, particularly because the French are always wooing neutral countries, and you know what kind of feed they can put on."

"You've been entertained by the French?"

"Would you believe President de Gaulle sent me a can of *foie gras* from his own backyard?"

"People really make a fuss over you, then."

"Why not? My vote is as important as Great Britain's in

the General Assembly, and as long as they don't know which way you're going to go, they have to cater to you."

"How do you finally decide which way you're going to vote?"

"I send a wire back home and ask them what we need. If they cable back that we need a dam, then I inform the Soviet bloc and the United States bloc, and I let them bid on it. The highest bidder gets the job and my vote."

"The highest bidder?"

"Yes, whoever offers us the most money is given permission to build our dam."

"That's one way of getting a dam built," I said.

"This doesn't happen every day. We really get most of our aid during an emergency session of the General Assembly. You can't get a ton of wheat during a regular session or, for that matter, a cup of coffee."

"I notice you're eating alone now. Does that mean no one is taking you to dinner tonight?"

"Not exactly. I'm eating alone, but the bill is being sent to Red China. Although they're not a member of the UN, they're so mad at the Soviet Union and the United States that they're trying to get me to abstain."

NEW HOPE FOR NATO

Now that France has pulled out of NATO, there is room for another country to come in. Several nations have been proposed for membership, but for one reason or another, their applications have been rejected. For example, in the case of Spain, the members have vetoed Franco's application on the grounds that the Spanish still condone bullfighting, which is against everything NATO stands for.

The most obvious candidate for membership in the North Atlantic Treaty Organization is the Soviet Union. The Soviet Union is strategically located, has a large standing army, which could cover Europe's northern and eastern flanks, and has several ports that could easily be used for supply depots.

NATO's main role in the past has been to contain the Soviet Union. But if the Soviet Union were permitted to join NATO, this would become a minor role, and our financial and military commitment could be cut in half without endangering European security.

Another advantage of having the Soviet Union in NATO is that the Russians already have nuclear weapons, so we wouldn't have to supply them with any. This would solve the major problem that the United States has had in dealing with its North Atlantic allies.

Besides its geographic location and its ability to field hundreds of thousands of troops, the Soviet Union could make a large contribution to NATO in the field of intelligence. The Western allies have been spending billions of dollars trying to find out what the Russians are up to. If they joined the NATO pact, we would have the right to ask them, and this would save us a tremendous amount of time and money.

Some critics argue that the Soviet Union already belongs to the Warsaw Pact, made up of the Iron Curtain countries, and it would be hard for the Soviets to withdraw from that pact to join ours.

But NATO has far more standing in the world than Warsaw, and it is believed the Soviets would not hesitate to jump over to our pact if somebody asked them.

Of course, if you took in the Soviet Union as a partner in NATO, you would have to change the strategy of the alliance. NATO would have to have a new military threat, or it would disintegrate.

That new threat could be France, and NATO's new role could be to contain General de Gaulle.

It is believed that with the Soviet Union in NATO, De Gaulle wouldn't dare try anything in Europe, and he would be convinced that any adventure on his part could mean instant retaliation, not only from the West but also from the East.

De Gaulle is going to Russia soon, and one of the things he's expected to do is to try to persuade the Soviets not to join NATO. But the Soviets are expected to turn a deaf ear to De Gaulle's pleas. The only promise De Gaulle can hope to extract from the Russians is that if the Soviets join NATO, France can take its place in the Warsaw Pact.

This column has not been cleared with the State Department.

AN ANTI-ANTI-MISSILE DISCUSSION

The Soviet Union and the United States are reportedly meeting in secret to discuss ways of not spending vast sums of money on anti-missile systems. The Russians claim to have developed such a system, and in the next few months Secretary McNamara has to decide whether the United States will build a system of its own, which would cost billions of dollars.

There is hope that some compromise can be worked out. I happened to be in a Washington restaurant and overheard one of the discussions.

The American diplomat said, "You must understand, Mr. Sergivich, that my country is prepared to go ahead with our anti-missile missile program, if your country goes ahead with yours."

"Aha, Comrade Smith," the Russian replied, "you cannot threaten us, because if you go ahead with your anti-missile missile program, then we will proceed with our anti-anti-missile missile plan, which will knock any anti-missile missile you develop out of the sky."

"I cannot give you the details," Smith said, "but we now have on the drawing boards an anti-anti-anti-missile-missile missile, which could destroy your anti-anti-missile missile before it even left the pad."

The Russian said, "I'll see your three anti-missile missiles and raise you one, that can knock a mosquito out of the sky."

The American looked at the Russian's poker face. "I think you're bluffing. I'll see your four anti-missile missiles and raise you two anti-missile missiles, making it a total of six altogether."

The Russian started to perspire. "Now let me get this straight. You're betting six antis and seven missiles against my four antis and five missiles."

"That's correct," Smith said.

"What if I told you we had an anti-anti-anti-anti-anti-anti-anti-missile-missile-missile-missile-missile-missile missile now in production?" the Russian said.

"And what if I told you that it doesn't bother us because we have an answer to it?" Smith said.

"You're cheating. You didn't say what it was."

"All right, I'll say it. Our answer is an anti-anti-anti-anti-anti-anti-anti-missile-missile-missile-missile-missile-missile-missile missile."

Smith could hardly catch his breath.

The Russian was smiling. "If you went ahead with that, we would have no choice but to go ahead with a weapon so powerful I hate to even think of it."

"And just what would that be?" Smith said.

"Do I have to tell you?" the Russian pleaded.

"If you don't, we won't believe you."

The Russian took a deep breath. "It's an anti-anti-anti-anti-anti-anti-anti-anti-missile-missile-missile-missile-missile-missile-missile-missile-missile missile," he said, gasping for air. The American gave him a glass of water, and the color started to return to the Russian's cheeks.

The Russian stared at the American. "Well, what is your response to that?"

"According to my calculations, you left out one anti-, so if you fired the missile, you would knock down your own weapons, instead of ours."

The Russian said, "It's impossible. I gave you nine antis and ten missiles."

"I counted," Smith said. "You only had eight antis. Why don't you try it again?"

"No! Not again," the Russian cried. "I'm sure our countries could work out some other solution."

BOMBS FOR SALE

There seems to be a shortage of bombs and other equipment from World War II which are needed for our present engagement in Vietnam.

Secretary McNamara revealed that the Defense Department had to buy back a number of 750-pound bombs from the Germans. The bombs were sold to the Germans for $1.70 each and bought back by the United States for $21 each.

The Pentagon isn't talking about it; but a worldwide search is going on for American war surplus, and just the other day a colonel showed up on the Island Mona Loren in the South Pacific, which had been an Army base in World War II.

He was greeted by the chief of the Mona Lorens.

"Welcome to Mona Loren, great white bird," the chief said. "We have not seen your kind since the savages of the Rising Sun threatened to engulf us with their yellow peril."

"Yeah, well, all that's forgotten now, chief. How's the old island doing?"

"The quonset huts are holding up well, but the tents are starting to leak. Have you come to give us more surplus?"

"No, chief, on the contrary, we thought we might move some of this junk out of here for you so you would have more room."

"To do what?"

"Put in urban renewal. That sort of stuff. Let me ask you, chief, you still got those bombs around that we left behind?"

"Oh, yes. Many bombs are still on the island."

"That's fine. I'm happy to tell you that we've been worried about your safety for the past nineteen years, and we've decided to remove them so no one will get hurt."

"Very good, smiling eagle. How much are you paying for them?"

"Well, we hadn't intended to pay for them, but I'll tell you what we'll do. We'll give you a box of chewing gum for each one we take away."

"Wait a minute, most honorable brass. The Germans were here a few weeks ago and offered us three dollars a bomb, FOB."

"Well, we'll give you three fifty a bomb just to show you there are no hard feelings."

"You are indeed generous, great white spit polish. But the French came a few days later and offered us five fifty a bomb, plus green stamps."

"This is ridiculous," the colonel said. "After all, they were our bombs in the first place."

"Yes, oh star-spangled friend, but the day your Army left our happy island to go Stateside, I asked the commanding officer as he got on board the boat what I should do with all the Army equipment, and I'd hate to repeat what he told me to do with it."

"All right, we'll give you seven dollars a bomb, and that's as high as we can go."

"Alas, dear uniformed liberator. The British were here just

two days ago and offered us ten dollars a bomb, plus a gross of Beatle records."

"Who else has been to see you?" the colonel said angrily.

"The Egyptians, the Israelis, the Cubans, the Malaysians, the Pakistanis, the Indians, the Greeks, the Turks, and the Rhodesians. The last bid on the bombs was forty-three fifty. Tell me something. What the hell is going on out there in the world?"

"Never mind. Okay, we'll pay you fifty dollars a bomb. And that's final."

"You have yourself a deal, proud brother."

"One thing more, chief. How much do you want for the skivvy shirt?"

LONG LIVE FRIENDSHIP

It was just by accident that the French-American Friendship League, composed of people who believe in strong ties between France and the United States, held a meeting in the same hotel as the Soviet—Red Chinese Brotherhood Society, made up of those who believe in maintaining closer ties between the USSR and Communist China.

Unbeknownst to either party, the meetings were held in adjoining ballrooms.

The French-American Friendship League started its meeting with a toast to what the chairman called "the two greatest powers in the Western world."

After the toast someone from the floor introduced a resolution attacking President de Gaulle's Cambodian speech in which he censured American policy in Vietnam.

A Frenchman jumped to his feet and said angrily that De Gaulle not only was right about Vietnam, but hadn't gone far enough in his attack on the United States.

An American delegate demanded the floor and said the United States would not be in trouble in Vietnam if it hadn't been for the bankrupt French colonial policies after World War II.

Another Frenchman got up and shouted that the Americans were responsible for U Thant's threat to resign from the United Nations.

An American yelled that De Gaulle had wrecked NATO and was taking all our gold besides.

In the meantime, the Soviet—Red Chinese Brotherhood Society meeting got under way with the chairman reading a paper praising the success of world Communism and predicting the decline and fall of Western imperialist nations. He told his audience that as long as the Chinese and Soviets followed the paths of true Socialism, American aggression would be defeated, and every capitalistic country would eventually be liberated by the people.

Following a standing ovation, a Russian writer got up and said he would like to condemn the Chinese Red Guard movement which attacked the Soviet Embassy in Peking and committed despicable acts against foreign Communist representatives.

A Chinese delegate rushed to the microphone and yelled that the Soviets had sold out to the Americans and were acting in tandem with the United States in trying to destroy the great thoughts of Mao Tse-tung.

A Soviet delegate pushed the Chinese speaker off the platform and said that it was the Chinese who, in the name of Maoism, were bringing the world to the brink of World War III and had perverted the Marxist-Leninist ideals of Communism.

Four Chinese delegates shouted from the floor that the Soviet Union had become a bourgeois counterrevolutionary society, which was threatening the borders of Communist China and would soon be dealt with.

While the French attacked the Americans in the Friendship League, the Chinese attacked the Soviets in the Brotherhood Society, and at almost the same moment both the Americans and the Soviets decided to walk out of their respective meetings.

The two groups happened to meet in the lobby of the hotel, and after several minutes of consultation they went into a third ballroom and started to draw up a charter.

And that's how the Soviet-American Friendship Brotherhood League Society came into being. Their first meeting is scheduled for next month.

FAREWELL TO ARMS

One of the subjects brought up for discussion between American and West German officials during Chancellor Erhard's visit to Washington was the purchase of American arms. It seems that in order to bridge the balance-of-payments gap, the United States wants the West Germans to buy more American arms. The West Germans don't really want to buy arms, as they feel they can't use them. The Americans maintain that if the West Germans don't buy our arms, we'll have to cut down the size of our troops in West Germany.

Let us listen in on a discussion between an American diplomat and a German diplomat that probably never took place —or then again, probably did.

"Mr. Spiegal, my government is very concerned about your cutback in ammunition and armaments order for 1966."

"Herr Jones, I have explained to you we don't need any more American guns and ammunition. We don't know what to do with the stuff we have already."

"Mr. Spiegal, it is not for us to tell you what to do with the guns we sell you, but my government is concerned with the flow of gold from this country. It's your duty as a free Western nation to buy as many arms from an ally as you possibly can."

"But Great Britain wants to sell us arms, too."

"Great Britain? Who defeated you in World War II? The Americans."

"But Great Britain held out all alone until you came into the war. We owe her something."

"We've had American troops stationed in Germany for twenty-one years. The least you can do is buy a few lousy tanks and airplanes."

"We're a peaceful nation, Herr Jones. We love everybody. Besides, those last American planes we bought from you kept crashing all the time."

"Mr. Spiegal, we have a brand-new plane that would be just up your alley. It flies three times the speed of sound, has air-to-air missiles, and is perfect for jungle warfare."

"Herr Jones, why should we need a plane for jungle warfare?"

"You never can tell when you'll get back one of your African colonies."

"Why couldn't we buy something else, a space rocket or a communications satellite? Why does it always have to be arms?"

"Because we must have a strong Germany if we're to keep peace in Europe."

"That's what got us in trouble the last time. Maybe we could buy LSD capsules instead?"

"Mr. Spiegal, I don't like to use hard sell, but how are you fixed in chemical warfare?"

"We can't give it away. Herr Jones, do you realize we have enough rifles and machine guns now to arm every man, woman, and child in West Germany?"

"Ah, but have you thought about the population explosion?"

"Couldn't we buy color television sets?"

"Mr. Spiegal, I must warn you that if you refuse to buy arms from us, we will have to pull all our troops out of Europe, and you will be forced to become a military nation."

"How could you do that to us? We wouldn't even know where to start."

WHY WE BOMBED MEXICO

In September 1967 a U.S. Pershing missile was test-fired from Utah. But it overshot its mark and landed in the town of El Cuervo, Mexico.

The Pentagon immediately announced that the firing was an accident and sent its apologies to the Mexican government.

In spite of the denial, there are some people in Washington who are not certain that the firing was accidental, particularly since it took place on the same day that U.S. warplanes bombed four hitherto untouched targets in the North Vietnamese port city of Haiphong. These circles insist that El Cuervo, Mexico, was one of the fifty-seven targets that the military has been insisting had to be bombed if we were to hamper supplies going into North Vietnam.

They say this is how the bombing of El Cuervo came about. Secretary of Defense Robert McNamara testified secretly before Senator John Stennis' Preparedness Committee, indicating that the Administration saw no reason to bomb Mexico at the present time. He said, "The bombing of El Cuervo would have little effect on supplies now getting into the hands of the enemy. Even if the bombing closed off all the Mexican routes, the Vietcong would find alternative ways of getting their matériel down the Ho Chi Minh Trail. Besides, the risk of confrontation with the Mexicans at this time far outweighs the military advantages of bombing the country. This is not only my decision but the President's also."

Chairman Stennis and his committee indicated that they were very dissatisfied with the Secretary's testimony and called several generals and admirals to refute McNamara's no-win policy.

The generals complained that their hands were tied by civilians in the Pentagon. An admiral told the committee, "Unless we are permitted to bomb the fifty-seven targets which are now off limits—of which El Cuervo, Mexico, is obviously the most important—we cannot win the war in Vietnam."

The Preparedness Committee was very impressed with the military arguments and issued a strong report rebuking the Secretary of Defense for not letting the Air Force and Navy bomb whatever targets they deemed necessary. "It is our opinion," the report said, "that as long as El Cuervo remains untouched, our military effort in Vietnam will be thwarted."

The difference of opinion between McNamara and his generals reached the press. To prevent it from becoming a public debate, the White House press secretary announced, "The President supports Secretary McNamara's testimony, and the Administration has no intention of bombing Mexico now. At the same time the President reserves his option to bomb it in the future if the North Vietnamese do not stop their aggression."

Two days later the Pershing missile was launched from Utah at El Cuervo. This immediately was interpreted by the press as a victory for the Pentagon brass and a defeat for Secretary McNamara.

But the White House didn't see it that way. An Administration spokesman said, "There is no rift between Secretary McNamara and the Joint Chiefs of Staff. The bombing of El Cuervo has been under consideration for some time, and under our selective target policies, the missile launching had the full approval of the President, the Secretary of Defense, and the Joint Chiefs."

When asked by a reporter if the bombing of Mexico was an escalation of the war, the spokesman said, "Absolutely not. The President has no intention of widening the conflict, and his only aim in shooting a missile at Mexico is to make Hanoi realize that the United States has no intention of getting out of Vietnam."

A reporter asked, "With the bombing of Mexico, there are now only fifty-six military targets that American warplanes still may not attack. Could you tell us what the next off-limits target might be?"

The spokesman replied, "Would you believe Expo 67?"

IS YOUR CITY WORTH SAVING?

The Joint Chiefs of Staff recently made a proposal to protect fifty U.S. cities from missile attack by defending them with the costly Nike-X antimissile system. The Pentagon said the cities were selected on the basis of size, but it turned out that many cities chosen were, in fact, smaller than those left off the list (*i.e.*, Charleston, South Carolina, population 76,000 and home of L. Mendel Rivers, chairman of the House Armed Services Committee, would be protected; San Diego, population 1,000,000 would not).

When Senators and Congressmen from unprotected cities heard about the list, they hit the Capitol dome, and some of them haven't come down yet. It's obvious that the Joint Chiefs' antimissile plan in its present form will never get through.

There must be a fairer way of selecting the cities that will get missile protection as against those that will have to be sacrificed in a nuclear war, and I've been giving it a lot of thought. Here are some of the ideas I'm running up the flagpole to see which ones the Joint Chiefs of Staff will salute.

The first thing would be to select twenty-five cities that have Democratic administrations and twenty-five cities with Republican administrations. In that way, after World War III, the United States could preserve the two-party system.

The next thing would be to select cities that are in good shape financially. It has to be assumed that after an all-out missile attack the country will have some economic problems, and there is no reason it should be burdened with additional financial difficulties from urban areas.

The cost of making fifty cities bombproof, according to the Pentagon, is in the neighborhood of $20 billion, which is quite expensive, and there may be some resistance from those taxpayers whose towns are not in the protected areas. But this is shortsighted, because it is economically unfeasible to save everybody, and those citizens whose cities cannot be protected will at least expire with the knowledge that their taxes kept so many of their fellow Americans alive.

There also may be people who live out in the country and suburban areas who might feel they have as much right to survive an atomic attack as the city folks, but here again they're taking the small view.

As an industrial nation, we need the cities for commerce, advertising, television, and mass transportation. Except for farmers, there's no one worth saving in the countryside. Besides, city people are so much better dressed than people who live out of town, that if you must make a choice in time of war, you have to go with the clothes-conscious city folk every time.

So the question boils down to which cities do you save? It could be left up to Billy Graham, Cardinal Spellman, or Bob Hope.

But if they couldn't agree, I think the best solution would be to hold a Miss Antimissile Contest on television.

Each city would send its most beautiful girl to Atlantic City, and she would be judged according to beauty, intelligence, and talent. The jury would select fifty girls as Miss Antimissile, and the cities they came from would be spared.

Another suggestion has been to give the Nike-X to any city with a professional football team, on the theory that people are going to need something to take their minds off the inconveniences caused by another world war.

THE HIGH COST OF MISSILES

It now appears the United States is going to build an antiballistic missile system. For the "thin" size system it's going to cost $3.5 to $5 billion; the "thick" one, which the military is opting for, will cost $30 billion.

When the news broke, my friend Cruxman called me and said, "Why do we have to spend five billion dollars to build an antiballistic missile system?"

"Because, Cruxman," I said, "the Russians are building one, and we have to have everything the Russians have."

"How do we know they're building one?" Cruxman demanded.

"Because they said they were building one," I replied, trying to be patient.

"Yeah, well, how come if we don't believe the Russians on anything else, we believe them when they say they're building an antisystem ballistic missile?"

"You mean an antiballistic missile system. Cruxman, you've got to understand that we would rather not spend the money, but we're being forced into it."

"All right. What about this? Suppose we announce we're building a system missile antiballistic, or whatever the hell you call it, and we stick up a bunch of old curtain rods and obsolete TV antennas and say, 'This is our defense, Boris, so don't go shooting any of your ICBM's toward North America.' "

"It's a good idea, Cruxman, but you forget one thing—the credibility gap. It's all right to lie to our own people, but we can't very well lie to the Soviet Union."

"How are they going to know we're lying?" Cruxman shouted. "As a matter of fact, how do we know they ain't lying?"

"Have you forgotten the Spirit of Glassboro so soon?" I asked.

"Yeah, well, let's just suppose," he said, "that they announced they were building their antiballistic system missile just so we would go ahead and spend ten to thirty billion dollars on ours.

"Now suppose, after we get it built, the Russians say, 'Ha, ha, you've wasted all that money because we don't have an antiballistic missile system. As a matter of fact, not only don't we have such a defense, but we've just discovered our antiaircraft barrage balloons don't even blow up so good.' Wouldn't that make us the laughing stock of the Western world?"

"Cruxman, you're only talking about thirty billion dollars. It's chicken feed."

"Let me ask you this question. They're speaking about a

'thin' ABMS to start with. What are they going to protect with it?"

"I imagine the major cities for a start."

"You must be kidding. By the time they build a defense system, there won't be a major city left standing in the United States."

"Why is that?"

"Because the cost of making the major cities livable comes to exactly the same price it costs to build a bunch of Nikes around them."

"Cruxman, wiser men than you have been wrestling with this problem for years. We would rather spend the money on other things, but we have no choice. We can't afford to let the Russians bomb our slums out of existence."

"Do me one favor," Cruxman begged. "Ask them over in the Pentagon, just for fun, if they'd stick up some curtain rods and old TV antennas over Omaha and see how the Soviet Union reacts. I'll lay you five to one they start putting up curtain rods and old TV antennas over Leningrad."

"All right," I promised, "but I don't think I'll have any luck. Once the Defense Department thinks it can get its hands on thirty billion dollars, it's kind of hard to make them let go."

12

⊠⊠⊠⊠⊠⊠⊠⊠⊠⊠⊠⊠⊠⊠⊠

GRAFFITI IS IN

FRESH AIR WILL KILL YOU

Smog, which was once the big attraction of Los Angeles, can now be found all over the country from Butte, Montana, to New York City, and people are getting so used to polluted air that it's very difficult for them to breathe anything else.

I was lecturing recently, and one of my stops was Flagstaff, Arizona, which is about 7,000 miles above sea level.

As soon as I got out of the plane, I smelled something peculiar.

"What's that smell?" I asked the man who met me at the plane.

"I don't smell anything," he replied.

"There's a definite odor that I'm not familiar with," I said.

"Oh, you must be talking about the fresh air. A lot of people come out here who have never smelled fresh air before."

"What's it supposed to do?" I asked suspiciously.

"Nothing. You just breathe it like any other kind of air. It's supposed to be good for your lungs."

"I've heard that story before," I said. "How come if it's air, my eyes aren't watering?"

"Your eyes don't water with fresh air. That's the advantage of it. Saves you a lot in paper tissues."

I looked around and everything appeared crystal clear. It was a strange sensation and made me feel very uncomfortable.

My host, sensing this, tried to be reassuring. "Please don't worry about it. Tests have proved that you can breathe fresh air day and night without its doing any harm to the body."

"You're just saying that because you don't want me to leave," I said. "Nobody who has lived in a major city can stand fresh air for a very long time. He has no tolerance for it."

"Well, if the fresh air bothers you, why don't you put a handkerchief over your nose and breathe through your mouth?"

"Okay, I'll try it. If I'd known I was coming to a place that had nothing but fresh air, I would have brought a surgical mask."

We drove in silence. About fifteen minutes later he asked, "How do you feel now?"

"Okay, I guess, but I sure miss sneezing."

"We don't sneeze too much here," the man admitted. "Do they sneeze a lot where you come from?"

"All the time. There are some days when that's all you do."

"Do you enjoy it?"

"Not necessarily, but if you don't sneeze, you'll die. Let me ask you something. How come there's no air pollution around here?"

"Flagstaff can't seem to attract industry. I guess we're really behind the times. The only smoke we get is when the Indians start signaling each other. But the wind seems to blow it away."

The fresh air was making me feel dizzy. "Isn't there a diesel bus around here that I could breathe into for a couple of hours?"

"Not at this time of day. I might be able to find a truck for you."

We found a truck driver, and slipped him a five-dollar bill, and he let me put my head near his exhaust pipe for a half hour. I was immediately revived and able to give my speech.

Nobody was as happy to leave Flagstaff as I was. My next stop was Los Angeles, and when I got off the plane, I took one big deep breath of the smog-filled air, my eyes started to water, I began to sneeze, and I felt like a new man again.

HOW UN-AMERICAN CAN YOU GET?

I have a confession to make, and the sooner it gets out in the open, the better I'll feel about it. *I don't drive a car.*

Americans are broad-minded people. They'll accept the fact that a person can be an alcoholic, a dope fiend, a wife beater, and even a newspaperman, but if a man doesn't drive, there is something wrong with him.

Through the years I've found it very embarrassing to admit it to anyone, and my best friends tend to view me with suspicion and contempt.

But where I really run into trouble is when I go into a store and try to make a purchase with a check.

It happened again last week when I went to a discount house at a large shopping center in Maryland. I wanted to buy a portable typewriter, and the salesman was very helpful about showing me the different models.

I decided on one, and then I said, "May I write out a personal check?"

"Naturally," he said kindly. "Do you have any identification?"

"Of course," I said. I produced an American Express credit card, a Diners' Club credit card, a Carte Blanche credit card, a Bell Telephone credit card, and my pass to the White House.

The man inspected them all and then said, "Where's your driver's license?"

"I don't have one," I replied.

"Did you lose it?"

"No, I didn't lose it. I don't drive a car."

He pushed a button under the cash register, and suddenly a floor manager came rushing over.

The salesman had now become surly. "This guy's trying to cash a check, and he doesn't have a driver's license. Should I call the store detective?"

"Wait a minute. I'll talk to him," the manager said. "Did you lose your driver's license for some traffic offense?"

"No, I've never driven. I don't like to drive."

"Nobody likes to drive," the floor manager shouted. "That's no excuse. Why are you trying to cash a check if you don't have a driver's license?"

"I thought all the other identification was good enough. I had to be cleared by the Secret Service to get this White House pass," I said hopefully.

The floor manager looked scornfully at the pass and all my credit cards. "Anyone can get cleared by the Secret Service. Hey, wait a minute. How did you get out here to the shopping center if you don't drive?"

"I took a taxi," I said.

"Well, that takes the cake," he said.

By this time a crowd had gathered.

"What happened?"

"Guy doesn't have a driver's license."

"Says he doesn't even drive. Never has driven."

"Lynch him."

"Tar and feather him."

"How un-American can you get?"

The crowd was getting ugly, so I decided to forget the typewriter.

"Never mind," I said. "I'll go somewhere else."

By this time the president of the store had arrived on the scene. Fortunately, he recognized my name and okayed the check. He was very embarrassed by the treatment I had received and said, "Come on, I'll buy you a drink."

"I forgot to tell you," I said. "I don't drink either."

This was too much, even for him, and he pushed me toward the door.

"Get out of here," he said, "and don't come back!"

MY WIFE, THE WRITER

Sometime last year, my wife decided to write a book with a friend of hers titled *White Gloves and Party Manners* aimed at the five to twelve-year-old jet set. In fairness to myself, I encouraged her in this endeavor, mainly to keep her off the streets as a den mother or a monitor in the PTA.

For several months she locked herself in the library with Marjabelle Young, and they turned out several drafts with the aid of a kindly editor.

Finally, they had the book in the shape the editor wanted, and the manuscript was shipped off to the printers for publication a few months before Christmas. I was pleased for her that she completed it and that a publisher wanted to print it, and I made a mental note to buy fifty copies just to assure her that her work had not been in vain.

What I didn't realize was that the book would take off and become a bestseller. The first, second, and third printings were sold out before Christmas, and book buyers all over the country were screaming for reorders. This happened at a moment when my own book had taken a slump in sales; but I must be honest and say I was very happy for her, and if I felt any pangs of jealousy, I took it out on the kids, not on her.

The bright spot, as far as I was concerned, was that it would give my wife some spending money, and she wouldn't have to come to me whenever she wanted something for herself.

Of course, I was wrong. A few weeks after the book was published, my wife said, "I need some money for a new suit."

"Why?" I wanted to know.

"I'm going on the *Today Show* to plug my book, and you can't expect me to wear an old suit."

I gave her a check for $150.

She came back two weeks later. "I have to buy another suit."

"You just bought a suit," I protested.

"I'm going on CBS-TV, and I can't very well wear the same suit I wore on NBC."

"Of course not," I said. "I'm a fool to have even thought of it." I wrote out another check for $150.

Two weeks later she was scheduled to attend an autograph party at Brentano's. "I suppose you'll need a new suit for the autograph party?" I said.

"No, but I could use new shoes and gloves and a hat."

A month had gone by, and I had spent about $500 clothing my wife for her book promotions.

Then she came in excitedly and said, "Neiman-Marcus wants me to go to Dallas and autograph books."

"Who is paying for your trip down there?"

"I didn't bother to ask," she said.

She came back after calling the store. "They said if I pay for the trip, they'll pay for my hotel room."

"You'll have to sell more books in Dallas than Truman Capote has in all of the United States to pay for your plane fare."

"You don't have to shout," she said. "I think you're jealous."

"I'm not jealous. The idea of writing a book is to make money. You can't use up your royalties tooting around the country signing books."

"Marjabelle said you'd say that," she said.

"And speaking of royalties," I added, "you're going to have to pay taxes on them, you know."

Her eyes narrowed. "What do you mean, taxes?"

"You earned the money—you have to pay taxes on it."

"That money is mine," she said firmly.

"But somebody has to pay taxes on that money, or I'll go to jail." I looked at her smiling. "You mean you'd let me go to jail?"

"Marjabelle and I earned that money. We worked hard for it. It's ours."

"Don't you see, if you don't pay taxes, I'll have to pay them?"

"That's between you and the government," she said. "Work it out any way you want to. Only Marjabelle and I are not giving up our royalties."

A month after Christmas I was out about $2,000 from *White Gloves and Party Manners*.

Then my wife came in and announced, "Marjabelle and I are going to write another book, and we're going to get a one-thousand-dollar advance from our publisher."

"I'll make a deal with you," I said. "I'll give you a twenty-five-hundred advance *not* to write it."

GRAFFITI IS IN

The graffiti craze (inscriptions or drawings scratched on pillars, buildings, and walls) is now in full swing in this country. Many have been made into buttons, a practice which has not only furthered the art of graffiti, but has everyone trying to think of new ones.

Time magazine held a graffiti contest, as a promotion, among advertising agency personnel throughout the United States, and these were some of the entries that were submitted:

"I dreamed I could wear a Maidenform bra"—Twiggy.

"Good night, David."
"Good night, Goliath."

"Hire the handicapped"—the Hathaway man.

"The Jolly Green Giant is a vegetable."

"Marshall McLuhan reads books."

"Xerox never comes up with anything original.
"Xerox never comes up with anything original."

"Drink Canada dry. Visit Expo 67."

"Do the Chinese look in the white pages?"

"Discourage ugly office buildings—play handball against the Pan Am Building."

"The Ajax white knight cheats at polo."

"Aunt Jemima is an Uncle Tom."

"Pall Mall can't spall."

"Smokey the Bear is a hairy Boy Scout."

While *Time* magazine has been concentrating on the advertising world, Washington has been working hard on its own graffiti. Liz Carpenter, Mrs. Johnson's press secretary, contributed several during a speech she gave at the Women's Press Club dinner, including:

"Bobby Kennedy is a rabbit."

"Secretary McNamara can't do New Math."

"Governor Romney—would you buy a *new* car from this man?"

"Keep smiling with Joe Alsop."

"Walter Lippmann—God is not dead. He's alive and appears twice a week in the Washington *Post*."

A multiple sclerosis charity ball in Washington last week used graffiti as its theme, and some of the signs said:

"Adam Clayton Powell uses Man Tan."

"Courtney Valenti (Jack Valenti's daughter) is a midget."

"J. Edgar Hoover sleeps with a night light."

"Richard Nixon is dead and living in New York."

One scratched out at the last moment was, "The Governor of Alabama is a mother."

Other graffiti now making the rounds of Washington are:

"Senator Dodd has never eaten a bad dinner."

"Impeach George Hamilton."

"General Westmoreland come back—you forgot to salute Senator Fulbright."

"George Wallace uses hair straightener."

"No, thank you, Dr. Coppolino, I've already had my shots."

"For Brotherhood Week—take your brother to lunch."

"Dean Rusk is a recorded announcement."

"Mrs. Johnson never waters the trees she plants."

"LBJ reads Walter Lippmann under the bedcovers."

"The U.S. has the answer.
"What was the question?"

TAKE ME ALONG

The airlines have a big push on to make wives fly with their husbands. United Airlines keeps singing day and night "Take Me Along," and TWA is really tugging at your conscience by printing full-page advertisements of a lonely brunette beauty with such copy as "Next business trip don't leave your heart at home."

It would seem to me that TWA should have learned its lesson by now. One of their executives told me that many years ago, when commercial flying was just getting under way, TWA was worried about women's fears of planes. So it inaugurated a plan allowing a man to take his wife free with him on a TWA ride anywhere in the country.

The response was excellent, and pretty soon TWA planes were filled with happy men and women holding hands and forgetting their fears together.

As a public relations follow-up, TWA sent a letter to one

wife a few weeks later, thanking her for flying with the airline and asking her to tell all her friends how safe it was.

This is where the whole program backfired. Many of the wives who received the letters had never flown at all. Apparently, their husbands had taken someone else along instead, and so while many mistresses were sold on flying, all the plan did was to get a lot of wives sore at TWA.

The husbands weren't too thrilled about TWA blowing the whistle on them either. So the plan was dropped, and it's taken forty years for someone to start a similar campaign again.

Since I travel a lot, I always encourage my wife to come with me, and I really don't need the airlines to push me.

About a week before I'm ready to leave on a trip, I say to her, "Why don't you come with me to Bladesville? I've got a big motel room, and they say it's very nice even during the pollen season."

"What are you going to do there?"

"I'll be working all day; but I'll be free around nine o'clock at night, and then we can go to dinner in the motel."

"But what will I do all day long?"

"I think there's a Sears, Roebuck store in town, so you could go shopping, and you could write letters in the lobby, and maybe they have a movie you could go to in the afternoon."

"It sounds very exciting."

"I'd also like you to meet an old friend of mine from schooldays. He and his wife are really wonderful people. They have six kids, and maybe you could keep his wife company while she's taking care of them."

"I can hardly wait to pack," she said.

"Take your boots with you. The roads are very muddy now during the monsoon season."

"Monsoons?"

"Oh, I forgot to tell you; Bladesville is right in the middle of the monsoon belt. A friend got stuck there for five days once because the airport was underwater."

"If it's all the same to you, I'd rather not go."

"Why not? You should get out. Besides, the worst that can happen while you're away is the kids could wreck the house."

"No, thank you."

"That's a shame. I hate to leave my heart at home."

THE FIVE-YEAR MARRIAGE

Since all our sacred institutions are under attack these days, it comes as no surprise to read that our concept of marriage has been challenged by a member of the American Psychological Association.

In a paper presented at a conference in Washington, Mrs. Virginia Satir, a psychological social worker from Big Sur, California, attacked the marriage vows people in the Western Christian world are forced to take. She said marriage is the only human contract in our society that has no time length, no opportunity for review, and no socially acceptable means of termination.

To expect people to make an unerring choice of a life partner is to ask them to be wiser than they can possibly be, she added.

Mrs. Satir's solution is a simple one. She advocates that marriage should be a five-year renewable contract.

If the marriage went well for the first five years, the couple could renew the contract for future five-year periods. If it failed, it would automatically be dissolved without undue stress, expense, litigation, or social stigma.

When I read the article, I naturally became very indignant and said to my wife, "Can you imagine? Some woman psychologist is advocating that marriage be based on a five-year contract, which is renewable only if both parties agree."

"Why do you bring it up?" my wife asked.

"Why?" I said, as I threw down the newspaper in disgust. "Because to me marriage is a sacred institution, and once you're married, you shouldn't have to decide every five years whether you want to continue it or not. Decisions like that could drive a man crazy."

"Then what you're saying," my wife said quietly, "is that you're not sure you'd be willing to renew the contract whenever a five-year period was up."

"That's not what I'm saying at all. In our case it would probably be automatic."

"Probably?"

"You're trying to put me in a corner," I protested. "Of course, it would be automatic, though if I am to be honest,

I'd have to admit that as the five-year deadline came near, I might give it more thought than I would under the present set of rules."

"Why is that?" she asked, with a grim smile on her lips.

"It's just natural. If people had options every five years, they would think about them. Marriage is a very serious business, and I'm sure you would think much less of me if I just signed a contract every five years without reading the small print. I'm not saying I wouldn't sign after I read it, but I might want to add a few clauses here and there that I hadn't thought of when we first got married."

"Such as what?" she said, as she straightened out the lampshade next to our bed.

"Well, I might put some ceilings on the spending of money, add a few paragraphs about your mother, and maybe include a freedom clause for myself. Things like that. But don't worry, there would be nothing in the contract that would stop you from signing it."

"Suppose I wanted to add a few clauses of my own?" she asked.

"What?" I said. "And wreck a perfect marriage?"

"It hardly seems worth discussing," she said, "particularly since it's doubtful that your psychologist friend's ideas are going to be adopted in the near future."

"I should hope not," I replied. "It would be a travesty in human relationships if, every five years, people had to decide whether they wanted to live together. You'd never be sure, after you signed, that you hadn't made a terrible mistake."

I didn't see the lamp coming until it was too late.

WHY JAPANESE MEN ARE HAPPY

American women could learn a lot from Japanese wives. Despite subversive attempts to liberate her, the Japanese wife is still a slave to her husband, who is her "only master on earth."

Not only has this made for happiness in the Japanese household, but it has also kept the divorce rate down to 10 percent, as opposed to in the United States, where 25 percent of all couples seem to find reasons to split up.

What are the major differences between the American and

Japanese woman? For one thing, the Japanese woman is much more concerned about the welfare of her husband. On cold mornings, for example, I was told a good Japanese wife will prostrate herself on her husband's side of the bed, so he won't have to step down on a cold floor.

It's small gestures like this that make for a solid marriage and a happy home.

Another area in which Japanese women excel is giving their husbands baths. There is an old Japanese proverb that "a family who washes together sloshes together," and anyone who has been bathed by a Japanese woman will never want to take an American shower again.

Unlike the American woman, a Japanese wife looks forward to giving her husband a bath. She stays home all day cooking the hot water so it will be just right when her husband arrives from a hard day at the office.

The wife will first bow to him and then help him off with his clothes. Then she'll start scrubbing him down with soap, making sure not to get any in his eyes. Finally, she'll rinse him off. Only then will she allow him into the bathtub, where he will soak up to his chin, while she serves him a cold beer or a hot glass of sake.

After the bath the wife will then massage her husband's back and even walk on him if he's really tired. Then she'll dry him off and dress him for dinner. By this time the husband is in a good humor and willing to listen to what the kids did in school.

Contrast this with the average American home, where the American wife not only refuses to bow to her husband when he comes home, but in some cases won't even give him a bath. And when she does gives him a bath, it's slam-bam thank you, ma'am, and about as romantic as a TV dinner.

Most American wives will run the water, hit their husbands a couple of times with a washcloth, and then hand them towels and say, "Dry yourself."

No wonder American husbands are irritable and hard to get along with at the end of the day. You would be, too, if your wife refused to walk on your back.

American women are afraid that if they offer to bathe their husbands, they will be considered inferior. This is ridiculous. A wife who knows how to bathe her husband in the Japanese style is a superior person and one whom any husband would be proud of stepping on when he gets out of bed in the morning.

13

✖✖✖✖✖✖✖✖✖✖✖✖✖✖✖

MEETING OF THE MINDS

THE ANTIPORNOGRAPHERS

Newsweek magazine has just done a cover story on the "Permissive Society." The article, illustrated with a nude Jane Fonda, deals with the great strides that have been made in the last few years with respect to sex in films, songs, fashions, and, of course, books.

Since you can't shock Americans anymore with sex, a new school of writing is now in the making, and I interviewed its leader, Malcolm McMoral. He is the author of the first antipornographic novel, *A Kiss on the Cheek*.

"Malcolm, I have read your book from cover to cover and didn't find one obscene word. Did you have a reason for eliminating all the dirty words or were you just trying to shock your readers?"

"Some reviewers have accused me of the latter; but the truth of the matter is my characters had no reason to curse, and therefore I had no reason to put obscene words in their mouths."

"Malcolm, in your book the title, *A Kiss on the Cheek,* is apparently taken from a scene on page one hundred fifty-seven where the mother kisses her eight-year-old son on the cheek. This is the only kiss in the book. Why?"

"Every writer has to deal with life, and that kiss was necessary for the development of the story. I didn't just throw it in for the heck of it."

"I'm not criticizing you for putting the kiss in. I'm criticizing you because there is absolutely no sex in the book at all. Do you think it's fair for people to pay five dollars and ninety-five cents and not have at least one really hot love scene somewhere in your novel?"

"All I can do is refer you to the Supreme Court decision of 1943 which says that you can publish a book without a love scene in it, provided it has some social value."

"So you justify your lack of love scenes in the book on the ground that it has social value?"

"Yes. Some dirty-minded people have accused me of writing a clean book for money. Well, I say: Who is to judge whether a book is clean or not? Sure, there are clean passages in it, but you have to have those if you're going to deal with reality."

"In your book the husband doesn't even commit adultery. Don't you think that's going a bit far?"

"Not in the context of the story. If you take it out of context, certainly it might sound that way. But the husband happens to be in love with his wife, and that's why people have said it's a clean book. There are a lot of cleaner books in drugstores now, so I don't know why my book should have been singled out."

"Yet your novel seems to be some sort of a breakthrough, and there is fear that other writers might start copying you, particularly if you prove there's money to be made in writing a clean book."

"That's not my problem. If I didn't do it, somebody else would have. Society is changing all the time. It's true that the clean novel is considered avant-garde at the moment, but that doesn't mean it's wrong. Someday there will be so many clean books on the market that no one will be shocked anymore."

THINKING THE UNTHINKABLE

It is not generally known, but among the brain trusts in our government is a man who probably has the most important job in the country. He is in charge of thinking the "unthinkable."

His name is Jean Pensepas, and his work is so secret that only a few close friends and associates know exactly what he is thinking.

How I got to see and talk to him is not mine to tell, but I was granted an interview and given permission to put down what he said.

Mr. Pensepas told me he first started working for the government early in the Eisenhower Administration, when it was unthinkable that we would get involved in a war in Southeast Asia. "While everyone else said it was unthinkable, I started to give it some thought. I concluded we ought to put some American advisers into Vietnam just to let the Vietcong know we meant business.

"In 1964 Barry Goldwater made some very strong statements about Vietnam," Mr. Pensepas said. "He advocated bombing North Vietnam, defoliating the Ho Chi Minh Trail, escalating American troops, and fighting the war until the enemy gave in. President Johnson said this was unthinkable, and he turned the problem over to me. Well, I thought and thought and thought, and I finally decided all these things weren't as unthinkable as the President thought they were."

"Do you think the President really thought they were unthinkable, or was he just saying it because it was an election year?" I asked.

"It's hard to tell about the President. He thought it was unthinkable that the machinists wouldn't settle the airline strike, and what he thought about the steel price raise was not only unthinkable but unprintable, so he might have been sincere in 1964 when he said that Barry Goldwater's proposals were unthinkable."

"But why did he change his mind?"

"I started thinking about it. All those unthinkable things Goldwater said made sense from a military viewpoint, and once the President felt Hanoi would not come to the conference table, he started to have second thoughts," Mr. Pensepas said.

"Do you think about unthinkable things after somebody does them?"

"Of course not. Once you do an unthinkable thing, it's not unthinkable anymore. For example, before we bombed the oil tanks around Hanoi and Haiphong, that was unthinkable. Now everyone takes the bombings for granted."

"What about Marshal Ky's suggestion that we invade North Vietnam?"

"At the moment that is still unthinkable, but just the other day former Vice-President Nixon said in Saigon that he didn't blame Marshal Ky for suggesting it. So it's really not as unthinkable as it was a month ago."

"Someone said that there would soon be a million Americans in South Vietnam. Is that unthinkable?"

"No, I wouldn't say it was. One thinks it is, until you study the statements of Dean Rusk and Robert McNamara, and then you start thinking otherwise."

"What is the most unthinkable thing you're thinking about now?"

"You mean if China comes into the war?"

"You're not thinking about using the—"

Mr. Pensepas smiled. "It hasn't been completely ruled out."

THE MAN WHO HATED BENEFITS

I am, as most people in Washington know, a very patient man. But there are times when even I lose my cool, and it usually happens in the winter, when everyone is giving galas and benefits for some worthy cause.

One day I came home from the office, and before I could take off my tie and splash some water on my face, my wife said, "We've been asked to go on the Committee for a White Tie Benefit they're giving for the Indigent Football Coaches Home in Rock Creek Park. Now before you explode, Eliza Stickler, the chairwoman, said we didn't have to do any work. They just wanted to use our names on the invitations."

I exploded. "You know that's just a way they're going to sucker us in."

"I knew that's what you'd say; but it's a worthy cause, and it's under the patronage of Mrs. Lyndon Johnson, Postmaster General Larry O'Brien, and all of Justice William Douglas' ex-wives. We really couldn't say no."

"Of course not," I shouted. "If we said no, we'd be taken out of the *Green Book,* and they'd cancel our credit at Avignone Frères."

"You're behaving ridiculously. There is nothing wrong with their using our name if it will help the Home for Indigent Football Coaches."

I forgot about the whole thing until three weeks later, when my wife said to me at supper, "Whom do you want to invite to the gala?"

"What do you mean, whom do I want to invite to the gala?"

"Well, since we're sponsors, we have to take a table for ten, so we can invite four other couples."

"How much is this little table going to cost?"

"It's two hundred dollars a couple, but before you get excited, it's deductible."

"Deductible from what?" I asked.

"I don't know," she said. "They said it was deductible, so we didn't have to worry about it."

"You know what it's deductible from?" I said. "It's deductible from the children's tuition, that's what."

"Oh, what's the difference? It's going to be a wonderful night. Eliza said they're going to have Danny Kaye, Sammy Davis, Jr., Frank Sinatra, and the Tijuana Brass for entertainment."

I ate my chipped beef and grits in silence. Two days later, right in the middle of the Washington Redskins—Baltimore game, my wife said, "Charlotte Possum just called, and she's on the raffle committee, and she said she was wondering if you'd ask Garfinckel's to donate a mink coat for the drawing."

"How can I ask Garfinckel's to donate a mink coat, when we haven't even paid our bill there for two months?"

"Well, Charlotte said they'd say no to her, but if you asked and they refused, you could write a nasty article about them."

"I thought we didn't have to do anything but lend our names to the committee?"

"What's wrong with asking Garfinckel's for a mink coat? Oh, by the way I need a check for one hundred and fifty dollars for the advertisement in the program."

"What have we got to advertise?"

"Nothing, silly. But I promised Eleanor Poolsinger—she's in charge of the program—we'd take an ad which would say 'Compliments of a Friend.' "

"You mean we can't even put our own name in the ad?"

"Now you know that would be very gauche."

Baltimore scored again, so I really can't say what depressed me the most.

The next night I came home, and my wife wasn't there. We waited until eight o'clock for dinner and then opened a can of chow mein. She arrived at eight thirty. "We had a meeting of the decorations committee," she said breathlessly. "And we're going to turn the Sheraton Park Ballroom into a football stadium with gold goal posts and blue velvet-covered stands. Lillian Sollaway knows this wonderful French decorator in New York who is going to come down and do it for us."

"It sounds wonderful. You got a call from the caterer. What's that all about?"

"Oh, I forgot to tell you. The committee asked me to give

a dinner party before the ball for all the African and Southeast Asian ambassadors and their wives. I think I ought to order some new drapes for the dining room."

I lost all interest in my chow mein. "This thing is kind of running into money," I said.

"A little; but it'll be fun, and you'll love the new dress I bought for the ball."

The day finally arrived, though it was hard to believe. Our dinner party of fifty was a huge success, and afterward we all went to the ball. Unfortunately Danny Kaye, Sammy Davis, Jr., Frank Sinatra, and the Tijuana Brass had previous commitments, and the entertainment was provided by a tap dancer from Hackensack, New Jersey; a singer, who was the sister of the chairwoman of the Entertainment Committee; and a Congressman from Texas, who did card tricks.

Two weeks later, thanks to Riggs Bank, I paid off all our personal debts.

I forgot all about the gala until one night I said to my wife, "Oh, by the way, how much money did you people make for the Indigent Football Coaches Home in Rock Creek Park?"

"I think it was thirty-nine dollars and fifty cents," my wife said hesitatingly. "It seems the decorations cost us much more than anyone thought they would."

THE TRUE SECRET SERVICE

The CIA has been getting so much publicity that one starts to wonder how secret our secret service really is. *Esquire* magazine devoted an entire issue to the CIA, The *New York Times* had a five-part series on it, and the CIA is defending an Estonian in a slander suit in Baltimore. In another case coming to court soon, a man who says he worked for the CIA is being tried for smuggling arms destined for Angola and Mozambique. You can't pick up a newspaper or magazine these days without reading about the organization.

Many people are bewildered over the amount of publicity the CIA is getting, but I can put their minds at ease. The reason the CIA is getting all the publicity is that it is *not* our major secret service organization. It is, in fact, a cover to detract from our *real* central intelligence agency, which is the Department of Agriculture.

Yes, the Department of Agriculture is the real intelligence organization, operating without fanfare, rarely getting its name in the papers and maintaining a discreet silence worthy of the greatest intelligence operation in the free world.

It can now be revealed that the CIA was set up for no other reason than to keep people from prying into the affairs of the Agriculture Department.

The $46,000,000 CIA headquarters at Langley, with its 16,000 employees, the far-flung spy network, the gathering of information from around the world are all a ruse that, up until now, has worked beyond the Department of Agriculture's wildest dreams.

The CIA has been blamed for the U-2 incident, the foul-up in the Dominican Republic, and the setting up of the Diem government in South Vietnam. What few people realize is that this is exactly the way Orville L. Freeman, the Secretary of Agriculture, wants it, because the more things the CIA gets blamed for, the less chance there is of discovering who was really behind these operations.

Whenever someone starts getting inquisitive about what the Department of Agriculture is up to, the CIA immediately leaks a story to the press of some momentous blunder the CIA committed, and everyone, including the Russians, thinks we goofed again.

The reason the Department of Agriculture was chosen to be our intelligence arm is that no one really cares what the Agriculture people do. They have an inexhaustible supply of funds that they are supposed to pay out to the farmers for not growing crops.

Using this as a pretext, the department can siphon off large amounts of money to its agents in the form of farm subsidies, and no one is the wiser.

Besides this, the department has crop-dusting aircraft, which are really used for spying operations, and all the storage facilities which are supposed to be holding surplus commodities are, in fact, filled with the latest and most sophisticated spy equipment.

The only time the Department of Agriculture was even remotely in the limelight was during the Billie Sol Estes swindle. But just when the heat was on, the CIA pulled off the Bay of Pigs caper, and everyone forgot about Estes.

The CIA angrily denied the charges that they were a front

for the Department of Agriculture when I called them. But the evidence is so overwhelming that their protestations just added to, rather than detracted from, my theory.

No organization that gets in the papers as much as the CIA could possibly be part of our secret service, and no organization that gets in the papers as little as the Department of Agriculture could be anything but a worldwide intelligence network.

Let this be a lesson to those who believe the United States government does not know what it's doing.

MEETING OF THE MINDS

The longer I live in Washington, the more impressed I am with how smoothly the government runs.

Not long ago I was in a government office, waiting to take a friend to lunch. He had just come out of a meeting and seemed pleased with how well it had gone.

"What was the meeting about?" I asked.

"I'm not sure what you mean," he said.

"Why did you have the meeting?"

"What a stupid question. What do you think we do in the government, just sit around and twiddle our thumbs?"

"I didn't mean that. What subject did you discuss at the meeting?"

"We discussed whether we should hold a conference or not."

"You had a meeting to discuss holding a conference?"

"Of course. And the consensus was that we should hold off on the conference until we meet again."

"Which, of course, will mean another meeting?"

"Now you've got it," he said. "I don't mind telling you I was pretty scared, because Agnew had called a meeting for ten o'clock, and Evans had called another meeting for ten thirty. Evans had no right to call the meeting without checking with Agnew, and when Agnew heard about it, he got pretty damned mad. So Evans moved up his meeting until eleven thirty."

"Did anything happen at Agnew's meeting?"

"We discussed in general the groundwork for Evans' meeting."

"Then by the time you met with Evans, you knew exactly what you were going to talk about?"

"We never got around to it because Wallaby, who had to make the major decision, was called to a meeting the Secretary was holding at the same time. Zimmerman was furious because he felt that he should have been invited to the Secretary's meeting, too, and he suspected Evans had called his meeting so Zimmerman wouldn't know about the other meeting."

"How did he find out about it?"

"Coates told him, rather maliciously, I thought. He expressed surprise that Zimmerman was sitting with us when Wallaby was across the street.

"Zimmerman said that he had met with the Secretary earlier, and the Secretary's meeting was just to confirm what they had gone over earlier. But Thurston told me later that the Secretary's secretary had told him not to mention the Wallaby meeting to Zimmerman."

"Did you ever find out what Wallaby's meeting with the Secretary was about?"

"Coates said it had to do with a meeting the Secretary is having in Washington next month. There was a conflict because several of the people the Secretary wanted had scheduled a conference, and the Secretary maintains there is no sense having the conference until they meet with him."

"You people in government meet a lot, don't you?" I said.

"We have to."

"Why?"

"Because if someone calls up my secretary and asks for me, it looks so much better if she says I'm in a meeting. How would you feel if when you rang me up, you found me in my office?"

"I'd feel you were stealing the taxpayers' money."

"Exactly. Now let's go have lunch. I have to be back at two o'clock for a you-know-what."

THE SUPER BOWL IN WASHINGTON

Americans have been subjected to so much football on television that it's very difficult for any of us to look at anything except in football terms. I couldn't help thinking as I watched President Johnson deliver his State of the Union message how it would have been reported by two football commentators.

"Good evening, folks, welcome to the Credibility Bowl, another wonderful State of the Union classic between the Great Society longhorns and the hard-hitting American solons, who haven't won a contest against the Great Society in three years.

"The backfield for the Great Society team is the same as last year. At quarterback for his third year is Lyndon B. Johnson, at fullback is Lyndon B. Johnson, at halfback Lyndon B. Johnson, and at flanker Lyndon B. Johnson. The line is composed of the famed seven blocks of Lyndon.

"The solons are fielding a strong defensive team of Republicans and Southern conservatives this year and are expected to give Great Society some serious opposition.

"Great Society has won the toss, and team captain Lyndon Johnson has elected to kick off and receive at the same time.

"Quarterback Johnson comes out of the huddle, takes the snap from center, and hands off the ball to the fullback, who hits the line for no gain. Halfback Johnson tries a run around end; but the rugged solon line is holding, and once again Great Society shows no appreciable gain. It's third down and long yardage. The quarterback rolls out to throw a long pass about taxes; but it's incomplete, and Great Society may have to kick.

"It's time out on the field, and seated next to me is one of the great experts of the Credibility Bowl classic, Asa Blotnik. Asa, how does the game look to you?"

"Well, Paul, these are two tough teams, and I think we're going to see quite a contest before it's over. Great Society had many injuries last November, if you recall, and I believe we're seeing the results of it here tonight. I notice that coach Johnson has decided not to try too many tricks and he seems to be more interested in consolidating his gains rather than trying any new plays.

"I talked to him just before game time, and he told me his team was in the greatest shape he had ever seen it; he pointed out they had made more yardage in the last three years than any previous coach had made in the last twenty.

"But he said this year was the time for testing, and if he didn't get support from the fans, his past victories would have little meaning."

"Asa, where do you think Great Society is the weakest?"

"I would say in the calling of the signals. The quarterback calls one play, and then they run another. Also, if you recall, a few years ago coach Johnson said he was going to concentrate on a ground attack. But lately he's been taking more and more to the air, and his strategy doesn't seem to be producing any results. Another thing that seems to be hurting Great Society is that many of the first stringers on the team are leaving or have left, and coach Johnson is having trouble trying to fill the positions. He seems weak in reserves."

"What about the American solons?"

"Well, you know they're always playing to the grandstands, and it seems this is the first year they feel they have a chance of holding the Great Society team down. As a matter of fact, this is the first time in the history of this game that Johnson's team has been forced to punt."

"Thanks, Asa, and now let's go back to the playing field. While we were talking, folks, there was an announcement over the loudspeaker that defensive back Adam Clayton Powell has just been kicked off the field for clipping and will be benched by the solons for the rest of the season."

THE APPOINTMENT OF LASSIE

The appointment of Lassie, the canine TV star, as special consultant to the Administration's Keep America Beautiful program has hit Washington like a bombshell. With the appointment of Betty Furness as Special Assistant to the President for Consumer Affairs, and now Lassie, President Johnson seems to have decided to recruit more television personalities to dramatize his Great Society programs.

The reason why the Lassie appointment came as a surprise was that most political observers here in Washington believed Lassie wanted to run for governor of California. Now that he's decided to work for the Administration, he may have hurt his political chances back home.

If the Keep America Beautiful campaign is a success, Mrs. Lady Bird Johnson will get all the credit. But if it fails, Lassie will be the one in the doghouse.

Sources close to the White House revealed that there was a foul-up concerning the appointment of Lassie. It seems that the President, who has promised to appoint more women to high government positions, had ordered his advisers to find a female dog to head his beautification program. Only after Lassie was sworn in was it discovered that the TV star was a male. The discovery was made when Lassie was introduced to the President's male collie, Blanco, in the rose garden, and nothing happened.

There were raised eyebrows among litterbugs, too, over the appointment of Lassie as a beautification expert. Critics have pointed out that just as Betty Furness never did her own shopping before becoming a consumer consultant (her cook did it all), Lassie has always had someone picking up his litter after him (usually a CBS vice-president).

But Lassie's supporters maintain that he's willing to learn everything there is about litter and that he's taking a crash course at the District of Columbia garbage dump to be filled in on his job.

This is not the first time that President Johnson has appointed a dog to his Administration. There have been others, in the State Department, Defense, HEW, and the Post Office. But so far this is the first dog associated with the beautification program.

The White House denied the appointment of Lassie was made to pay off a political debt. A White House spokesman said, "Lassie was picked up on his merits, and he has the full support of the American Kennel Association. The President knows he will make a contribution to the United States, and to show that the appointment was not merely for show, he is upgrading Lassie's position and will let him sit in on Cabinet meetings."

There may be some Senate opposition to Lassie's appointment, mainly from friends of the billboard lobby, who feel that dogs have done more damage to billboards than anyone else. But Senate supporters plan to defend Lassie on the grounds that his bark is worse than his bite.

Lassie was not available for comment, but close friends said that he jumped at the chance to serve his country.

A close acquaintance told me, "Lassie has vowed to run a clean administration, and he isn't going to be pushed around. When he gets his teeth into something, he doesn't let go."

Asked if he supported President Johnson's policies in Vietnam, the acquaintance said, "Lassie would never bite the hand that feeds him."

THE SECURITY CHECK

The Senate Internal Security Subcommittee recently released classified material involving the security clearance of eight distinguished American citizens. It was unevaluated material gathered by Otto F. Otepka, and many people protested that this kind of thing harked back to the McCarthy era.

I didn't realize how dangerous something like this could be until I was interviewed by a security specialist from one of the government agencies, who was checking up on a good friend of mine who was being considered for an important job.

We shall call my friend Bill Hoganblatt, and I knew him from my days in Paris.

The security man was very friendly. "How long have you known Hoganblatt?" he asked me.

"About eighteen years," I replied. "I want to say he's one of the finest men I've ever had the pleasure to be associated with. He's a good father, a kind husband, a loyal friend, and a great American."

"What kind of people did he associate with during the years in Paris?"

"All kinds. Writers, artists, businessmen. Bill was a very democratic guy."

"Were there any left-wingers among these friends?"

"Come to think of it, I think there were. At least some of them had strong political convictions, but I don't believe Bill —then again he never did say much about politics."

"Didn't you find this strange?" the investigator asked as he took notes.

"I didn't at the time, but now that you mention it, there was something funny about Bill's not wanting to discuss politics."

"You said it; I didn't. What about his drinking habits?"

"As far as I know, he never touched the stuff at all."

"Then you'd call him a secret drinker?"

"Come to think of it, he probably was. I never trusted a guy who wouldn't drink in public."

"What else can you remember about him?"

"He used to go to the museums in Paris a lot."

"Did you ever see him go to a museum?"

"No, he just said he did."

"Then he could have gone anywhere during those times. Even to the Soviet Embassy."

"By golly, he could have. I wouldn't have put it past him."

"One more question. As an American citizen, would you want Hoganblatt to work for your government?"

"I should say not! I didn't realize what a contemptible rat he was until I talked to you. For all I know, he's another Alger Hiss, and I hope he gets what's coming to him real soon."

WHAT'S IN A NAME?

As if there isn't enough trouble in the world, a British doctor by the name of Trevor Weston discovered not long ago that people are suffering from an "alphabet neurosis." He claims people whose last names begin with the final eight letters of the alphabet, S through Z, have three times as many heart attacks as those whose names begin with the letters A to R.

Dr. Weston says he believes the reason for it is that the people at the bottom of the alphabet are always at the bottom of the list, always waiting for their names to be called. Since they first face this in school, the S to Z children are filled with anxieties that carry through to their adult years.

I was very skeptical of Dr. Weston's theory, so I decided to see if there was any basis for it.

I went into a bar and asked a man sitting on a stool what his name was. He looked frightened. "Why me?"

"Don't be frightened, sir. I'm just taking a survey for my newspaper."

"Stevens," he said. "George Stevens."

"May I buy you a drink, Mr. Stevens?"

"I'm only drinking milk. I have a bad ulcer. It's killing me."

"That's very interesting. How did you get it?"

"Arkin and Blauvelt gave it to me. They're in my advertising agency, and they're out to get me."

"Why do you think they're out to get you?"

"They got Thomas, Unrum, Young, and Vogel. I'm the only one left except for Zimbalest."

"Where's Zimbalest?" I asked.

"He had a heart attack, his third this year. God knows, I'll probably have one myself soon." He started biting his nails.

"I didn't mean to shake you up so," I said.

"It's not you. I'm trying to get the courage to go home. You see, I was up for a promotion today, and I thought I'd make vice-president. Carstairs made it, Douglas made it, Eberhardt made it, Franklin made it, Gregory made it, Hofstatter made it, Iselin made it, Jacoby made it, King made it, Logan made it, Mankowitz made it, Nolan made it, O'Brien made it, Potter made it, Robertson made it, and that was it. They said there were no more VP positions open."

"That's a shame," I said.

"I guess I can't complain. Tait, Upjohn, Verick, Washington, Xavier, Yale, and Ziegenthaler were let go."

"Were they given any reason?"

"Allenby, the president, said they couldn't stand the pressure. They were always blowing up in front of the clients. Ziegenthaler thought everyone was out to get him, and they were."

"If you're under so much pressure, why don't you quit?"

"I can't. My kids are in so much trouble in school, I need the job. Say, you're not a friend of Abernathy's, are you?"

"No, I'm not."

"That's good. I think it was Abernathy who gave me my second ulcer. Either him or Donovan. They killed Zilch, you know. Say, by the way, what kind of survey are you taking?" he asked.

"I'm trying to find out if the people whose last names begin with the letters *S* to *Z* are more insecure than those whose names start with *A* to *R*."

"Why, that's ridiculous!" Stevens said, as he swallowed three tranquilizers. "What will they think of next?"

14

※※※※※※※※※※※※※※※※

EXPLAINING THE SYSTEM

A BOOST UP A STUMP

One of the problems of the election year 1966 was the emphasis placed on who was the President's man and who was Bobby Kennedy's man in a local contest. When a Bobby Kennedy man is defeated in a primary, it is considered a blow to the Kennedy machine. When a Johnson man loses, it is a defeat for the President's policies in Vietnam.

Even a coroner's election has national implications for the politically starved press, and we can expect to see more read into the results of the 1966 elections than the forefathers of the Democratic Party ever dreamed of.

If the truth be known, many of the local candidates are trying to disassociate themselves from both Kennedy and President Johnson, and they live in fear that either of these national figures will show up to campaign for them. But what do you do when you get a telephone call from Washington late at night at your local campaign headquarters?

"It's the President," the campaign manager whispers, holding his hand over the phone.

"Tell him I'm out making a speech," the candidate says.

"Congressman Klinker is out campaigning, sir. He should be back in a couple of hours. Oh, you'd like to come out and make a few speeches for him?"

"Tell him with the airline strike, he can't get here," the candidate says.

"You forgot he has his own airplane," the campaign manager says.

"Tell him it's impossible to get a hotel room. There's a Shriners' convention in town."

"Sir, this is the Congressman's campaign manager, and I know he'll be thrilled with your decision. But our last poll shows the Congressman will be a shoo-in, and we feel it might be better if you campaigned for somebody who really needed it."

The campaign manager turns to the candidate. "He says he has nothing to do next weekend, and he thought he'd like to visit our part of the state just to keep his hand in."

"Tell him next weekend is very bad. They're expecting tornadoes out here."

The campaign manager speaks into the phone again. "Yes, sir, I am still here. You'd be willing to appear at a fund-raising dinner? Well, I know this is hard to believe, but we have too much money now. We're going to have to give some back. Oh, you would be? Just a minute." He turns to the Congressman.

"He said he'd like to give a major policy speech on Vietnam in your district."

"Oh, no." The candidate holds his head. "Tell him he'll be picketed."

The campaign manager turns to the phone. "Yes, sir." He whispers, "He says if you don't want a speech on Vietnam, how about a humdinger on civil rights?"

"Tell him we've got the civil rights vote."

"Yes, sir. Well, I'll have the Congressman call you as soon as he comes back. We're most grateful, sir." The campaign manager hangs up.

The campaign manager says, "What are we going to do now?"

"Let's not panic," the candidate says.

The phone rings again, and the campaign manager picks it up. "Who?" He turns to the candidate. "It's Bobby Kennedy. He says he has nothing to do next weekend and would like to visit our part of the state."

"Okay," the Congressman says, "let's panic."

NEW CAMPAIGN TECHNIQUES

In politics it isn't how you play the game, but who attacks you that counts. Witness a recent tour of George Wallace. Wallace had been touring the North for a few weeks and had been getting far more television and newspaper coverage than any husband of the governor of Alabama deserved.

It wasn't what he said that attracted the attention (he's been using the same speech in every town), but the fact that he had been picketed, heckled, and in some places even shaken up by hostile crowds.

These scenes, which are made for television, provided Wallace with far more exposure than he ever hoped to get and gave every politician a new type of campaign to work for in the future.

In 1968 a politician and his staff will be talking something like this:

"Well, chief, we've got everything lined up for you on your Midwest tour. They'll be throwing tomatoes at you in Columbus, there will be a sit-in in Toledo, they'll walk out on you at Ann Arbor, and they'll overturn your car in Detroit."

"Wonderful, McNally. It sounds like a great tour. By the way, we seemed to be awfully short on hecklers in Pittsburgh. As a matter of fact, I was afraid I'd have to finish my speech."

"Sorry about that, chief. We had about one hundred hecklers all lined up, but the police wouldn't let them into the building. I explained to the police captain that you couldn't start speaking without them, but he just laughed at me."

"Well, let's see that the police get the word from here on out. Now, am I supposed to be shoved in Cleveland and mauled in Louisville or shoved in Louisville and mauled in Cleveland?"

"We think it would be better if you were mauled in Cleveland. We've arranged it for them to set fire to your car in Grand Rapids, and then if this were immediately followed by mauling in Cleveland, you'd make both the *Huntley-Brinkley* and *Cronkite* shows the same night."

"Okay, but see that my suit gets torn this time. I looked awfully clean after that riot in Lincoln, Nebraska."

"Don't worry, chief. Listen, we have a surprise lined up for you at Harvard next month."

"What is it?"

"All the students and faculty are going to walk out on you."

"What's so special about that?"

"During the Yale-Harvard football game?"

"Hey, that isn't bad. I'll be the only one left in the stadium. If that doesn't get me on the tube, nothing will. Are you still planning to have a bomb threat when I speak at Vassar?"

"Bomb threats don't seem to mean anything anymore, chief. We've got to give them the real thing."

"Okay, but let's not overdo it."

"Now, chief, we've got one more problem to resolve. You can say no if you want to, but I think this would help your image tremendously in the Southeast. We can get a good buy on some tar and feathers in Buffalo, and we thought during your speech—"

"Let's wait on the tar and feathers until later, boys. We don't want to blow all of our good stuff in the primaries."

THOUGHTS OF A CANDIDATE'S WIFE

It is regrettable that when the wife of someone running for public office is interviewed, she can't say what is really on her mind. In order to be a good candidate's wife, she must show a stiff upper lip and stick with the standard clichés about her husband, her home, and her children.

Now, for the first time, thanks to a new extrasensory perception process, I can reveal what is really going on in the mind of the wife of the candidate. Her thoughts are in italics:

"Mrs. Goodfellow, what is the most important role a wife must play in her husband's political career?"

"She must give him moral support when he is discouraged. She must be his ears and eyes when he isn't around, and she must be able to make him relax at the end of a hard day's campaigning."

As well as keep him off the bottle and away from all the skirts who think he's God's gift to women.

"You have four children. Do you find they miss their father when he is out making speeches all the time?"

"I imagine they do. But Charlton's a wonderful father, and he always makes time for the children, no matter how many political commitments he has."

Would you believe he hasn't seen them since the Fourth of July?

"Do you find the children understand that both of you have to be away from home so much?"

"Oh, yes, they're wonderful about it, and they're as interested in the race as we are."

They've only run away from home twice—the second time they asked to be placed in an orphanage.

"Do you get upset at the terrible things that are said about your husband during the campaign?"

"Oh, no. One must understand that politics is a rough business, and I'm used to it."

But if I ever see the wife of the candidate Charlton is running against, I'll scratch her eyes out.

"Mrs. Goodfellow, do you find it is tiring to be constantly in the limelight and always on your best behavior?"

"I love it. When we first got married, Charlton indicated he wanted to go into politics, and I knew that although it would place me in the spotlight, our lives would be exciting, thrilling, and rewarding. I wouldn't change my life for anything."

Except to be married to a plumber or somebody else with a respectable job.

"How do you manage to keep so beautifully dressed all the time?"

"I make do on Charlton's salary. You just have to know where the bargains are."

If it weren't for the trust fund Daddy left me, I'd be in rags right now.

"Mrs. Goodfellow, do you ever get any time alone with your husband?"

"Oh, yes. We steal many hours together and talk about the children and the funny things that have happened during the campaign and the intimate day-to-day happenings of our lives."

The only other people present are his political campaign manager, his press man, his finance chairman, and forty-three other volunteer workers.

"Mrs. Goodfellow, if your husband wins his race for office, will you change your living habits in any way?"

"Oh, no. I'm going to be the same person I was before."

I'll just take more tranquilizers instead.

HIS OWN MEDICINE

After suffering a defeat at the hands of Congress over Medicare, American physicians are taking an active interest in the 1966 political campaigns. The *Wall Street Journal* reports that not only are many distributing literature in their waiting rooms (mostly Republican and conservative pamphlets) but the doctors are also going out ringing doorbells. This display of political action is having varied results.

Not long ago my friend Block received a call from his physician in Maryland, and the doctor asked if he might stop over and discuss the elections with Block at his home.

"I'm sorry," Block replied gleefully. "I never let doctors make house calls."

The physician persisted, and Block finally said, "Wait a minute, I just had a cancelation. You can come over to see me at six o'clock Friday night."

The doctor showed up exactly on the hour, but when he rang the doorbell, Mrs. Block answered it. She led him into the living room and handed him a copy of a 1964 *National Geographic*.

"Please make yourself comfortable," Mrs. Block said. "My husband will be with you as soon as he can."

Forty-five minutes later Mrs. Block returned and said, "Mr. Block will see you now."

Block was seated behind his desk in the library. "Sorry about keeping you waiting, Doctor," he said, "but I just had an emergency. Now what seems to be the trouble?"

"I came to discuss with you the local election situation."

"*Hmmnn*, I see," Block said, taking out his fountain pen. "Now let me get some background first."

"Background?"

"Yes. Have you had any political problems in the family? Mother, father, grandparents, sisters, brothers?"

"Not that I know of," the doctor said, completely bewildered.

"When did you first start feeling you had to go out and do something about the elections?"

"As soon as Medicare was passed. I said I was not going to see this country go down the Socialist rathole of Europe."

"Are you getting enough sleep?" Block asked.

"Of course, I'm getting enough sleep. Now if you'll just let me explain to you the position of my candidate."

"Not so fast, Doctor. We'll get to that in due time. I notice you seem to smoke a lot. How many cigarettes do you smoke a day?"

"A pack a day. What has that got to do with what we're talking about?"

"I have to get the whole picture," Block replied. "I also note you're overweight. Is that a drinking problem or a will-power problem?"

"A little of both. Dammit, Block, are you going to let me talk to you about the campaign or not?"

"Follow my pen with your eye, Doctor. *Hmmnn*. Now try to touch your toes. *Hmmnn*. All right, now open your mouth wide."

The doctor was becoming furious. "Block, I'm a busy man, but I've decided to devote several hours to getting the right people elected to Congress."

"All right," Block said. "Now take off your shirt, and we'll have a close look."

"What for?"

"I just want to see if in your heart, you know you're right."

"OK, Block, it's obvious you're not interested in hearing the other side. I'm sorry I bothered you."

"Just a minute, Doctor—that will be ten dollars."

"Ten dollars? This is an outrage!"

"Listen, if I had to go to your house to discuss politics, I would have charged you twenty. You're lucky I could see you at home."

EXPLAINING THE SYSTEM

It is very hard for a resident of Washington, D.C., to explain the American election system to a foreigner. A representative of South Vietnam came here not long ago to study our elections so he could go back to his country and report on how the greatest democracy in the world works.

Let us call him Tri Vang Vin.

"Whom are you going to vote for on Tuesday?" Tri Vang Vin asked.

"Nobody," I told him. "We're not allowed to vote."

"But how can that be?" Tri Vang Vin asked. "Is this not the capital of the United States?"

"Exactly," I replied. "That's why we're not allowed to vote. You see, anyone who lives in Washington, D.C., may vote only once every four years for the President of the United States. The rest of the time on election day we have to stay at home."

"But who represents you in Congress?"

"Everybody," I said. "A Congressman from South Carolina might tell us how much money we can have for schools, a Representative from Nevada could dictate how much in taxes we have to pay, and a Senator from West Virginia will tell us what kind of police department we can have. We're too dumb here to think for ourselves."

Tri Vang Vin said, "How can you be a democracy if you cannot decide for yourselves who will represent you?"

"Oh, we are a democracy, all right. That's why we don't have the vote. You must understand that the question of home rule for Washington has been debated many times, and it's always been defeated because Congress claims that if they gave the eight hundred thousand citizens of Washington the right to choose their own government, it would be unconstitutional."

"But the people in Washington always keep telling us that we must allow the people of South Vietnam to vote."

"That's true. They want the people of South Vietnam to have the vote, but they don't want the people in Washington to have a say in their own affairs. You see, Congress trusts you, but they don't trust us."

"Why not?"

"Because Congress likes to run Washington, D.C. If they gave us home rule, they wouldn't be able to fix their own traffic tickets."

"Ah, that I can understand. But if this is true of your capital, why couldn't we decide not to let anyone in Saigon have the vote?"

"Our Congress would never stand for that," I said. "We're pouring a lot of money in there, just so all the people in South Vietnam can decide their own destinies. If you disenfranchised Saigon, your elections would be a fraud and a mockery."

"But why aren't your elections a fraud and a mockery, if eight hundred thousand people in the nation's capital have nothing to say about their destinies?"

"Because we're not a backward nation. We have spent billions of dollars persuading everyone in the world that the only solution to their problems is free and open elections. And this country believes that everyone should have the God-given right to vote, except, of course, those people who live in the District of Columbia. You see, my friend, the United States has to draw the line somewhere."

15

※ ※ ※ ※ ※ ※ ※ ※ ※ ※ ※ ※ ※ ※ ※

DOLCE WHITE HOUSE

THE THREE BEARS

Linda Bird Johnson has just written an article for *McCall's* magazine on how she announced her engagement to Captain Chuck Robb of the U.S. Marine Corps. In the article she tells that she crawled on her hands and knees into her mother's bedroom at three in the morning and, finding her mother gone, crawled into her father's bedroom, woke them both up, got into bed with them, and announced she was going to get married. So help me. I didn't make a word of this up. It's all there in *McCall's* for everybody to read.

And then there were these three bears.

There was Papa Bear, Lady Bear, and Lynda Bear.

One night they came home, and Papa Bear said, "Someone's been sleeping in my bed."

Lady Bear said, "Someone's been sleeping in my bed."

And Lynda Bear said, "Someone's been sleeping in my bed."

Papa Bear said to Lady Bear, "How do you know someone's been sleeping in your bed?"

"Because I was sleeping in *your* bed."

"And how do you know someone's been sleeping in your bed?" he asked Lynda Bear.

"Because I looked for Mama in her bed, and then I looked for her in your bed, and then I got into bed with both of you."

"Well, then, who slept in Mama's bed?" Papa Bear asked.

"You did," Lady Bear replied. "You said the Lincoln bed wasn't big enough for three people."

"That's right. I did say that. Okay, but who slept in Lynda Bear's bed?"

"I did," said Lady Bear.

"Why?" Papa Bear demanded.

"Because you were sleeping in my bed."

"That's right, Papa. None of us did get too much sleep."

"Let's get this straight," Papa Bear said. "I slept in Mama's bed, Mama slept in Lynda Bear's bed, and Lynda Bear slept in my bed."

"That's correct, Papa. It drove the Secret Service bears crazy," Lady Bear said.

212

"What I don't understand," Papa Bear said, "is why Lynda Bear couldn't sleep in her own bed."

"Because I'm going to marry Chuck Bear and I wanted to tell you about it. Don't you remember?"

"All I remember is seeing you down on your hands and knees, and the thought occurred to me you should be walking upright. You're a big bear now."

"I was just pretending I was a baby bear," Lynda Bear said. "Like I used to be when I was little."

"That's right, Papa," Lady Bear said. "Don't you remember how she used to crawl to us when she had something to tell us?"

"I suppose so, but let's get tonight squared away. Who's going to sleep in whose bed?"

"You sleep in your bed, Papa, I'll sleep in my bed, and Lynda Bear will sleep in her bed."

"Won't the other bears think that's kind of grizzly?"

"Who would tell them?" Lady Bear said.

Lynda Bear said, "I have to. I'm writing a piece on the hibernating of bears for *McCall's* magazine."

THE INTELLECTUAL VOTE

It has been widely reported that President Johnson is very concerned about his inability to get through to many of the country's intellectuals.

Since the President wants to be loved by all the people, he has been asking members of his immediate Administration family what he can do to get the intellectuals on his side. He even had a luncheon for sixteen of his own house intellectuals to discuss the problem.

The luncheon was, of course, off the record, so an outsider can only use his own imagination as to what went on.

"Now, gentlemen, Ah called you all together today to break bread with me and discuss a very pressing problem. How can we get the blankety-blank intellectuals in this country to see mah side of things?"

"Well, Mr. President, I think it's more a question of image than anything else. May I speak frankly?"

"Not too frankly, son."

"Intellectuals just don't believe anyone from Texas can

communicate with them. They look down on you as a country boy who is more at home driving around his ranch at ninety miles an hour than he is reading the collected poems of T. S. Eliot."

"It was eighty-five miles an hour, and you know it."

"That isn't the point, Mr. President. The point is we've got to make you into an intellectual so that the intellectuals will consider you one of them."

"That's a hot one. How do you propose to do that?"

"Well, I thought we might get Jim Bishop or William S. White to reveal what you like to read at night before you go to sleep."

"What do Ah like to read at night before Ah go to sleep?"

"For a start, I thought we might say Plato, St. Thomas Aquinas, Shakespeare, Tolstoy, Kafka, Camus, and the poems of Allen Ginsberg."

"They'll never believe it," the President said. "Mah Daddy said you can fool some of the intellectuals all of the time and all of the intellectuals some of the time, but you can't fool all of the intellectuals all of the time."

"Well, what about this, Mr. President? Suppose we announce that as a hobby you've taken up writing poetry. We could release a poem every so often that you wrote in your spare time."

"It's not a bad idea, but who are we going to get to write the poems?"

"How about Robert Lowell?"

"Forget it. What other bright ideas do you people have?"

"I was thinking, Mr. President, that you might invite Leonard Bernstein instead of Martha Raye down for your next party. The intellectuals think a lot of Leonard Bernstein."

"Wal, Ah think a lot of Martha Raye. And besides, Leonard Bernstein can't sing 'Hello, Dolly.' "

"You probably will think this is a little far-out, Mr. President, but have you ever thought of growing a beard? Intellectuals trust anybody who has a beard."

"Lady Bird would never hear of it. And besides, Ah might antagonize the hawk vote."

"Sir, perhaps you could start buying up paintings by Jackson Pollock, Paul Klee, and Andy Warhol."

"Why, that's the ugliest thing you've suggested so far!"

"Mr. President, I think it's a mistake to try to woo the intellectuals. I believe you should just be yourself. After all, anyone can be an intellectual, but how many people can be President of the United States?"

"Now you're talking, Marvin. Have another helping of barbecued ribs."

THE PRESIDENT'S PORTRAIT

It seems a pity that after all President Johnson has done for the arts, the least the artists could do is paint a decent portrait of him. Sometime ago it was revealed that the President angrily rejected artist Peter Hurd's commissioned portrait of him as "the ugliest thing I ever saw." Mr. Johnson, whose taste in paintings leans more toward Norman Rockwell's magazine style, objected to the Hurd portrait on the grounds that it was too large, the Capitol Building in the background was too prominently lit and "inappropriate," and the positioning of the figure and the general style were not consistent with other White House portraits.

Many people, including art critics and museum directors, have come to the defense of Mr. Hurd, but as has been the case lately, very few people have come to the defense of the President. I wish to be included in the minority.

I believe the President had every right to reject a portrait of himself if it didn't fit the image he has of himself. The likeness of the President, as I saw it in photographs, leaves much to be desired.

In Mr. Hurd's portrait the President seems to be looking off dreamily into the distance as if searching for a consensus or a friendly Congressman. His lips are set as though he has just had a conference with a group of Democratic governors. His chin looks as if he's just heard a report from Ambassador Ellsworth Bunker on Vietnam, and his nose looks as if he's just smelled another resignation from his White House staff.

The suit he is wearing is dark and conservative with a vest, giving the impression the President might be a wealthy real estate man or a successful television station owner, and the book he is holding in his hand looks as if it could have been written by Arthur Schlesinger.

But forgetting the portrait for a moment, anybody could see why the President would object to the way Mr. Hurd positioned the Capitol in the background.

Anyone who knows the President's personality should have been aware that the only way to pose the President in such a picture was to have him *standing* on the Capitol itself with one foot on the Senate and the other on the House of Representatives.

Also, if Mr. Hurd had studied his subject more closely, he would have painted the light shining over the Capitol coming from the President's face and not from within the Capitol itself.

In the commissioned portrait President Johnson objected to the size of the Capitol, which is one-sixth the size of the President. The implication can be clearly drawn from the portrait that the Capitol plays a great part in the President's life, when anyone who lives here knows the exact opposite is true.

I think Mr. Hurd owes it to the President to try again. He could start by showing the President smiling. Instead of a book, he could be holding a 1964 Lou Harris or George Gallup opinion poll.

And instead of the Capitol, Mr. Hurd could paint in the LBJ ranch or the Pedernales River.

Many museums are bidding for Mr. Hurd's portrait, but I think it would be unfair if it were publicly displayed, particularly when people know the President doesn't approve of it.

You can say anything you want to about President Johnson's taste in art, but at least he knows what he likes.

NO YES-MEN IN THE WHITE HOUSE

The immediate reaction of most people when they heard that Bill Moyers had resigned from the White House was that there wouldn't be anybody left in the Administration who would stand up and say no to President Johnson.

There are many in Washington who believe that President Johnson will now be surrounded with nothing but yes-men, but an unnamed White House aide denied emphatically that this was true.

He told me, "There are many of us who work in the White House who say no to the President three and four times a day, and he respects us for it."

"Could you give me an example?" I said.

"Well, just yesterday, I was in the President's office, and he said to me, 'Do you think my popularity is slipping as much as the polls indicate?' And I said, 'No, Mr. President, I don't think it is.'"

"That's amazing," I said. "And he didn't get angry?"

"He did not. He respected me for saying no to him."

"Could you give me another example?"

"Well, last week one of the people in the White House went to the President, and the President said to him, 'I hope you haven't planned to spend Christmas with your family,' and this person retorted without hesitation, 'No, Mr. President, I hadn't.' Now does that sound like a yes-man to you?"

"It certainly doesn't. It takes courage to say no to the President of the United States."

"These are just two isolated examples," the aide said. "But it happens every day. No President wants his staff to agree with him all the time. Why, a few weeks ago we had a meeting, and the President asked our frank opinion on what we thought about a tax raise. One aide said, 'Yes, Mr. President, I think there ought to be one.' And the President said, 'I don't like yes-men on my staff.' So the aide immediately said, 'No, Mr. President, I don't think there should be one.'"

"Things like that give you faith," I had to admit.

"You must understand," the White House aide said, "that you're not doing a service to the President or the country if you agree with him all the time. I recall when I first started in this job being ushered into the President's office, and the President said to me, 'Do you think Ah can please all of the people all of the time and still be a great President?' And I said, 'No, Mr. President, I don't think you can.' And he said, 'If there's anything Ah hate, it's a know-it-all.'"

"That's a side of the President no one ever hears about," I said.

"Sure, we're going to miss Bill Moyers," the White House aide said, "but there isn't one of us who isn't willing to fight for what we believe in, if we have the facts. Only a few weeks ago the President asked one of us down at the LBJ ranch, 'What's the speed limit in Texas?'

"The aide replied, 'Seventy-five miles an hour,' and the President said, 'Ah thought it was ninety miles an hour.' But the aide said, 'No, Mr. President, it's seventy-five miles an hour.'

"The President said, 'Would you split the difference with me and call it eighty-five miles an hour?' The aide agreed, which proves Mr. Johnson is willing to compromise, even if he knows he's wrong."

Just then the phone rang, and the aide picked it up. "No, Mr. President . . . of course not, Mr. President. No, sir . . . nope . . . no, and I'll say no again. Of course, you're the President, but it's still no."

He hung up perspiring.

"What was that all about?" I asked him.

"The President wanted to know if I sent Bobby Kennedy a Christmas card."

THE NEW JOHNSON IMAGE

Now that President Johnson's operation on his throat has been so successful, I can reveal the reason the President decided to have it done.

It had been no secret that the President's popularity has been slipping. Despite the fact that he had got more legislation through than any other President and although the country was riding its greatest wave of prosperity, many people seemed to be voicing suspicions of their leader. The President, who rules by consensus, was smart enough to know that something had to be done about his image. But what?

He called in all his advisers just before he left for Manila and laid it on the line. He wanted them to speak frankly and make any suggestions that they thought would make the people love him again.

One adviser said, "I think we should put more stress on presenting you as a statesman and less on the fact that you're trying to think of new ways of spending the taxpayers' money."

Another adviser said, "Mr. President, your popularity was at its height when Luci got married. Couldn't you arrange a Christmas wedding for Lynda?"

"Ah probably could," the President said, "but that would give us all of 1967 with nothing to do."

A third adviser said, "Mr. President, you asked us to speak frankly, and I will. A recent poll taken by Zlonk Brothers asked people what was the one thing that annoyed them the most about your television appearance, and seventy-three percent of those questioned said it was your Texas accent."

"Well, what am Ah supposed to do about that?" the President said angrily.

"Now don't get mad, Mr. President. I'm just quoting the poll. Perhaps if we could change your accent, we could change your image."

"It's a little late for that," the President flushed.

"No, it isn't, sir. There's a doctor at Johns Hopkins who can perform a minor operation on your throat which could change your speech overnight. He can give you any accent you want."

The President said, still angry, "And what accent do Ah want?"

"I was thinking of a New England accent, with perhaps a slight Harvard twang."

"Never," the President said, slamming his fist on the conference table. "Ah was born in Texas, raised in Texas, and Ah love Texas."

Just then an adviser came in with the latest popularity polls. They revealed the President had slipped two percentage points.

The President studied the polls for several minutes and then said, "Will the operation hurt?"

"No, sir. It's just like having a polyp removed. I assure you, sir, with your dynamism and a New England accent, you'll be unbeatable."

"What about Lady Bird?"

"People like her accent, so she won't have to do a thing."

"Of course," another adviser said, "if you did have the operation, you'd have to sell the ranch."

"Then where would Ah go on vacation?" the President shouted.

"They say Hyannis Port is very nice in the summertime."

"All right, all right. But if it doesn't work, there's going to be some very sorry people around here."

"Don't worry, it will work, Mr. President, and I can't wait to see the expression on Bobby and Teddy's faces when you give your State of the Union Message to Congress in January of next year."

THE BATTLE OF FOUNDATIONS

Among the many distinguished committees I serve on without pay is the National Kidney Foundation, which supports and encourages research into the incidence, causes, treatment, prevention, and cure of all kidney diseases. Other people on the honorary campaign committee are Mrs. Hugo Black, Mrs. Dwight D. Eisenhower, Mrs. Arthur Goldberg, Senator Jacob Javits, and Mrs. Earl Warren.

Now a foundation depends on publicity, and naturally we all were excited, sometime back, when the President was going to have a kidney stone removed. We figured kidneys were going to come into their own, and the President might even be willing to serve on the committee, if not as an adviser, at least as a doctor.

But President Johnson's propensity for piggyback surgery is well known, and he never seems to be satisfied with one operation when he can have two for the same price. Some people feel his approach to surgery is nothing more than an extension of his economy moves, best exemplified by his desire to turn off all the lights in the White House.

Anyway, in a few moments the whole public relations campaign for the Kidney Foundation was geared up for the President's kidney stone operation, and there were even some optimists who thought we might become more famous than the Kinsey Foundation, which of course does research in other work.

But the President, or perhaps his doctors, threw us a curve and decided to remove a gallbladder at the same time. The gallbladder is located way up north and is not even remotely connected with the kidneys in any way. And as luck would have it, the President's gallbladder got all the publicity.

While this pleased the National Gallbladder Foundation, it caused havoc at the National Kidney Foundation headquarters. We tried to save the day by briefing newspapermen on the seriousness of the kidney stone removal and were making some headway when the President himself decided to show reporters and photographers his gallbladder incision in what has now become one of the great newspaper pictures of the Johnson Administration.

The National Kidney Foundation immediately demanded equal time, but President Johnson ignored us completely and pleas for him to show his kidney scars fell on deaf ears.

In the most recent series of operations, the National Kidney Foundation was on the sidelines, and the fight for newspaper space and TV time was between the National Polyp Foundation and the National Gallbladder Foundation. It was no contest—the Polyp Foundation won hands down, and the gallbladder coverage was buried in the bottom of the stories filed from Bethesda Naval Hospital.

Now the gallbladder people know what it's like to share a President's operation with somebody else.

But things are looking up at the National Kidney Foundation. While President Johnson has not given his personal endorsement to our work, his press secretary has agreed to go on the Kidney Foundation's honorary committee.

We feel the President has come over to our side, because Moyers has had a medical history of ulcers, but no kidney trouble. Therefore, we all reason, Moyers must have joined our foundation at the President's request.

WHO WILL SWIM FOR LBJ?

It has been reliably reported by Peking Radio that 500,000 civilians and soldiers swam the Yangtze River near Wuhan early this month to celebrate the triumph of Mao Tse-tung's thoughts and principles.

It was a magnificent gesture on the part of the Chinese people to honor the revered chairman of their Communist Party. The thought then occurred to me that since so many people were on vacation in August in the United States, perhaps some of them would like to swim for President Johnson. I didn't expect to get 500,000 people at the outset, but I must admit I was hoping to get more people than I finally did.

I started recruiting swimmers on the island of Martha's Vineyard, where I was staying for the month. I went down to the beach and said to several friends, "Anybody for a swim?"

About six people said they would like to go in.

"Before you go, I'd better warn you that this isn't an ordinary swim. What we're doing is swimming for President Johnson to celebrate his great triumphs of the past year."

All six sat down again on the sand.

One swimmer said, "The water's too cold."

Another added, "I've got a cramp."

A third person, who had at one time worked for the President, said, "I just ate lunch."

"Now that's no way to be," I said angrily. "Five hundred thousand Chinese swam for Mao, and the least we can do is show President Johnson we support him with the same fervor."

"Would it be okay if I treaded water?" someone asked.

"No," I said. "You've got to swim. Look, if we swam from Vineyard Haven to West Chop shouting President Johnson's thoughts as we went, it would not only be great for the President, but we'd feel better, too."

"How do we know what President Johnson's thoughts are?" was the next question.

"We could shout slogans from his speeches," I said.

"Such as?"

" 'We're winning the war in Vietnam,' 'Governor Romney can't control his people,' 'Go to church on Sunday,' and 'Your President is doing the best he can.' "

"I hear there are jellyfish in the water," someone in the crowd said.

"Excuses, excuses," I cried in anguish. "Our President is facing insurmountable problems, and the whole Communist world believes this country is torn asunder. One lousy swim for President Johnson would show the Commies that on the big questions America is united."

"Couldn't we snorkel instead?"

"No, no, no. We've got to swim."

"I don't want to get my bathing suit wet."

"All right," I said. "But someday in the future, when you're all working as busboys in a Red Chinese country club, I hope you'll remember the day you refused to swim for our leader."

"I have an idea," one of the party said. "Why don't you go across the sound and see if you can recruit some swimmers for Mr. Johnson over on Cape Cod."

"Where?" I asked.

"Well, you could try Hyannis Port for a start."

THE TRUE McNAMARA STORY

The debate over whether Secretary Robert S. McNamara jumped or was pushed out of his Defense Department job goes on unabated in Washington. McNamara watchers were caught flatfooted when a London bank teller leaked that the Secretary of Defense had been nominated to head the World Bank.

One student of Great Society upheavals was still kicking himself this week when he told me, "I should have known something was wrong when Captain Chuck Robb didn't select McNamara as his best man for the Lynda Bird wedding."

All sorts of stories about how President Johnson and Secretary McNamara agreed to part have appeared in the newspapers and on television, and as usual I'm the only one who got the inside scoop.

It has been known for some time that Secretary McNamara and former screen star Shirley Temple Black disagreed on the strategy of conducting the Vietnamese war. Shirley has wanted to mine Haiphong Harbor, bomb the center of Hanoi, and go for all-out victory against the enemy. She has been supported in her position by the Joint Chiefs of Staff.

Secretary McNamara, on the other hand, has been more cautious than Shirley, hoping to eke out some sort of settlement short of blowing up all Southeast Asia.

President Johnson was somewhere in the middle. Although he respected his Secretary of Defense, the Shirley Temple solution sounded more appealing as each day went by.

The President would have probably let things ride as they were, except for a casual conversation he had with McNamara a few months ago. The President asked him: "Bob, where do you do your banking?"

"I have a friend at the Chase Manhattan," the Secretary of Defense replied.

"Have you ever thought of putting your money in the World Bank?" the President asked. "I understand if you open an account there before January, you get a free set of dishes."

McNamara said, "I have the greatest respect for the World Bank, and I sure could use a free set of dishes; but I don't know anybody over there."

"I know George Woods, and I'll give him a call tomorrow."

"Gosh, Mr. President, you don't have to do that."

"Don't be silly. It's no trouble. Besides, if I get someone to open an account there, I get a free set of dishes, too."

President Johnson made a call to the World Bank the next day and talked to Woods. Much to his surprise, he discovered that not only was the World Bank short of depositors, but it was looking for a president as well.

Suddenly President Johnson got an idea. Instead of just opening an account for McNamara, he'd make him president of the World Bank. In this way Mr. Johnson could show his appreciation to his Secretary of Defense and at the same time have a friend there in case the United States ever needed a loan.

The President decided to spring the announcement on McNamara as a surprise, so he didn't mention a thing about it. Secretary McNamara had forgotten about it, too, and went about his business, hoping he could cool down Shirley Temple.

Then one day in London some loudmouth told a reporter that McNamara was going to be the new head of the World Bank.

The President was chagrined because he wanted to break it to the Secretary himself on Christmas morning. (The appointment was going to be inserted on a Christmas card and delivered to Secretary McNamara with the set of dishes.)

Unfortunately, when the story leaked, the President had no choice but to confirm to McNamara that, indeed, he was going to be the new president of the World Bank.

Secretary McNamara gulped and said, "But all I wanted to do was open an account there. I didn't mean to head it up."

"Bob, you should know by now when your President does something, he does it with style."